FROM
TIP TO TOE

gestalten

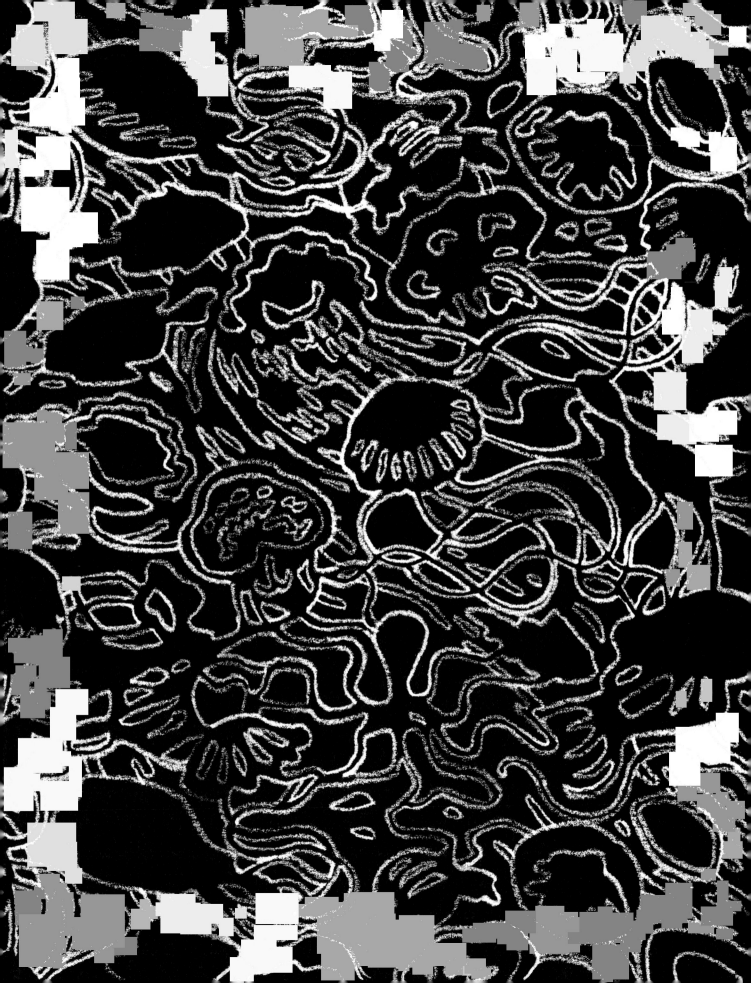

CON
TENTS

TABLE OF
CONTENTS

INTRODUCTION

FASHIONS FADE, STYLE IS ETERNAL

by
DUNCAN CAMPBELL

Style is that elusive fox—a notion that is often discussed, dissected, sought, and cultivated, but so rarely mastered. As one peels back the layers of what has become a ubiquitous idea, constantly examined and re-examined through the lenses of context, trends, and history, it still has the power to elude the pursuer. Ives Saint Lauren once said „Fashions Fade, Style is eternal" though to learn what style is, or what makes a man stylish, you need to muse on the themes of fashion, masculinity, the roles of gender, and the power these give to the holder.

Style can raise the ordinary man up and give him the power to command a conversation, a company, or even a country.

Perhaps what makes style so engaging a subject is that there is no single definition, and by its very nature, what works for one man with a sense of assuredly effortless insouciance may come across as contrived on another. It is the wholly personal nature of the beast that makes it so ripe for comparison from one man to the next, and so irresistible a subject for brands to tap into. As we continue to live ever more of our lives online, the link between men's style in its physical and digital iterations

Style can raise the ordinary man up and give him the power to command a conversation, a company, or even a country.

has never been stronger. Street style blogs continue to multiply at an exponential rate and today the excitement generated outside a fashion show has no trouble rivaling what's going on inside. Now more than ever, style is no longer something merely to be enjoyed, but also to be captured, compared, and collated. Whether this is an improvement on the past is open to discussion, and there are certainly those who think this new era of scrutiny is a symptom of our selfie-obsessed times. But whichever camp you fall into, it does mean that it's never been easier to learn about and appreciate men's style.

Now more than ever, style is no longer something merely to be enjoyed, but also to be captured, compared, and collated.

The subject of style icons is an interesting one. If you asked a gathered dinner party for a list, it's likely that the same names and images would appear again and again. Lord Byron perhaps, Marlon Brando in a white t-shirt, Fred Astaire, Bryan Ferry, Paul Newman astride his famous motorcycle, Gianni Agnelli certainly, or David Hockney grinning in a bow tie. All of these men, to one degree or another, lived certain aspects of their lives as a performance. Whether in a literal sense as an actor or musician, or in some more abstract way—creating characters for themselves as a means of emancipation or rebirth. These are men remembered for their style, but defined in their own lifetimes by their actions, their art, their leadership, and their characters. Of course, there's probably more to life than style when we think of the bigger picture, but it's not a bad place to start.

What's interesting with these stylish men is that few people today would want to look just like them. The famous Thomas Phillips portrait of Lord Byron in traditional Albanian dress completed in 1813 has something faintly ridiculous about it, but there's no denying that the man himself looks rather stylish. Famously protective of his own image, Byron even went so far as to instruct his publisher John Murray to destroy engravings of himself that he didn't like, ensuring that his aesthetic legacy was just as he intended. Perhaps it's reassuring to know that someone went to such lengths to control the way they were perceived by the world, as it means we don't have to. Everyone talks about the Duke of Windsor and how good he looked. And it has to be said that the man knew how to wear a suit. Whether he was good at anything else, however, is another question entirely.

So if it's not the physical aspects of the style we admire, then what? Perhaps it's more to do with the confidence that an assured sense of style implies. It's as if each one is saying, "This is how I have chosen to be seen by the world, and we both know it works, so let's leave it at that." And of course there's the all-important aspect of appearing like you haven't given it all that much thought at all. *Sprezzatura*, apart from being a wonderful word, is a charismatic concept that has seen a resurgence in recent years. The Italian trick of making the difficult look easy, being on just the right side of wrong. Gianni Agnelli was certainly the master of this craft, whether it was wearing his watch outside his shirt sleeve, leaving his tie blade longer at the back or sporting hiking boots with a suit, he is the undisputed king of elegantly studied nonchalance. Which is not to say, of course, that these tricks would work for everyone, but rather that they make up part of a larger whole—an attitude, a sense of fitness for purpose and knowing what the rules are and how to break them.

Sprezzatura: **The Italian trick of making the difficult look easy, being on just the right side of wrong.**

What, then, do these stylish characters have in common? Is there a red thread that links the stylish in all their many guises? Confidence, certainly, is part of the picture. Confidence in oneself, and also in one's sartorial decisions. The idea of a uniform is also an important one. Sometimes in a literal sense, but more often as a kind of self-imposed signature that becomes the trademark of the stylish man. Whether it's David Hockney's bright colors, Bryan Ferry's wide-lapelled Savile Row suits or James Dean's motorcycle jacket, a uniform can be composed of a single item, or a whole look, but the effect is the same. It allows the wearer to cut a consistent silhouette, recognizable without being formulaic, and hopefully without ever having to think too much about it.

Like being able to mix a proper drink, tie a bow tie, and catch a fish, there are some things that the stylish man should know how to do well, and chief among them is know how to dress himself.

One important style signifier, perhaps belonging to a dying breed of gentleman, is the secure knowledge of what to wear and when. The intricacies of morning dress perhaps, or the difference between white and black tie. Obviously as time goes by, these rules evolve, lose relevance, and disappear, but I think there remains something charming about a man who knows just how to dress, whatever the occasion—whether a sailing trip in Sardinia, a hike in Yellowstone, or a night at the opera. Like being able to mix a proper drink, tie a bow tie, and catch a fish, there are some things that the stylish man should know how to do well, and chief among them is know how to dress himself.

There is a particular skill in knowing what to wear—how far to push the boundaries of a dress code to appear distinctive and stylish, while remaining within the confines of the occasion. It goes without saying that some of this responsibility falls on the host to let their guests know what is expected, but an important caveat to this point should be noted. In the same way that too much shared knowledge on a subject can turn someone quickly from an engaging aficionado into a bore, so too can the self-appointed style expert be too quick to give his opinion on a perceived faux pas. While compliments on another man's style are most welcome, criticisms should probably be kept to oneself.

Whether you argue that style is something innate or learnable, the modern man needs in his arsenal a dependable set of sartorial tools that will see him through any occasion and through the changing seasons of the year.

Whether you argue that style is something innate or learnable, the modern man needs in his arsenal a dependable set of sartorial tools that will see him through any occasion, from day to night, from casual to formal, and through the changing seasons of the year. While some would argue there can be no substitute for the feeling of a beautifully crafted bespoke suit and the way it floats almost above the body, molding to the contours and improving the shape where necessary, this is far from the only option. *From Tip to Toe* is about the bigger picture, and creating a look and feel that is greater than the sum of its parts. Exactly what these parts should be is a source of debate but, in general, questions of fit, detail, quality, and suitability are a good place to start, closely followed by a sense of relaxed confidence and always remembering not to take things too seriously. The following book contains a carefully curated collection of brands and makers who all embody this spirit in one way or another. Some have long and storied histories while others bring new thinking to the table, but what they all share is a sense of quality, honesty, and élan that won't let the stylish man down.

INTRODUCTION

COUNTRYWEAR

COUNTRYWEAR

THE ROAD TO TWEED

IT WAS ONCE A STRICT RULE THAT GOOD STYLE
YIELDED TO PRACTICALITY AND PROTECTION. NO LONGER!
TODAY'S COUNTRYWEAR FASHIONS SKILLFULLY MELD
HERITAGE AND INNOVATION.

by
OMAR MUÑOZ CREMERS

In spite of the continuing growth of cities, modern man remains fascinated by nature. Ours is still a romantic conception of nature and on weekends or holidays, many of us seek out the calming effect of beach, forest or mountain. But the joy of nature can be disturbed by the surprising cruelties of bad weather. With nature becoming a popular leisure destination a new sense of fashion was embraced during the 20th century, consisting of garments that offered protection against the elements and the strain of walking. The outdoors style did not have to be colorful or fashionable; practicality and shielding were of the utmost importance. Over the years, countrywear nevertheless attracted the interest of bold fashion designers who aestheticized the style. At the same time, the interest in new fabrics has traditionally rivaled that of sportswear. The tension between heritage and innovation makes countrywear at the beginning of the 21st century an exciting and versatile style.

The roots of what we now call countrywear or outdoors fashion lie for the most part in work clothing, especially those garments worn by workers who confronted the elements every day. Many professions used natural fabrics that had

The tension between heritage and innovation makes countrywear at the beginning of the 21st century into an exciting and versatile style.

been known and processed by hand for centuries. Probably the most influential workwear is that of the fisherman, who in Northern regions—where wind, cold temperatures, and seawater combine—often has to work under extreme conditions. The essential garment for every fisherman used to be the sweater. While in France and around the Mediterranean a thinner version was worn—the white cotton marinière with its characteristic 21 blue stripes—fishermen of the North Sea and Atlantic Ocean preferred a rugged sweater made of wool, which provided insulation and water resistance. Many of today's premium brands specializing in woolen sweaters, like Inis Meáin, S.N.S. Herning and Guðrun & Guðrun, use original models worn by fishermen and are often located in communities where the traditional knitting craft has survived.

From the mid-19th century on, the invention of materials, machines and procedures would result in a new generation of garments offering workmen durable and reliable protection. The vulcanization process was quickly applied to the production of rubber boots while an English company called Barbour started to make

coats of waxed cotton which offered fishermen unparalleled water resistance. Both garments would grow into pillars of the British countryside style, which demanded protection from frequent precipitation. Typical countryside activities like horse riding, gardening, hunting, hiking, and bird spotting were provided with specialized gear and interpretations of coats and rubber boots like the green Wellington by Hunter Boot, which became a true outdoor classic. Continuous urbanization made the outdoor style look increasingly archaic, almost eccentric. Some garments did at first profit from the influence of military gear; Barbour for instance still carries coats that were largely designed during the Second World War. The duffle coat, a popular urban alternative to the waxed coat, was also introduced as part of the naval uniform. After the war, British company Gloverall purchased large quantities of surplus coats and started to produce its own version of the duffle coat, adding the characteristic leather loop fastening with Buffalo horn toggles. The parka-length coat became a rage in the 1950s and 1960s after which it lost its popularity for some time.

Today one of the keywords in menswear is heritage. Heritage is a subtle alternative to the broader nostalgia that seems to have a firm grip on large parts of contemporary culture. Nostalgia undoubtedly caused the revival of the duffle coat and changed the fortunes of Gloverall, one of many semi-forgotten or unfashionable brands that have made a comeback in recent years. Swedish newcomer Stutterheim evokes the past in a different manner by offering rubber raincoats in a minimalistic cut, a slightly updated recreation of a brandless model from the 1960s that no professional fisherman would wear these days. The handmade Stutterheim Alhorma is a perfect example of workwear turning into everyday clothing, a synthesis of functionality and aesthetics. While heritage does entail a fascination with older models, it also encompasses brands that show a renewed interest in manufacturing clothes by hand, often using natural and local textiles in the country of origin. These choices do have some consequences for heritage brands: often production is done on a smaller scale, inevitably resulting in higher prices for customers. While the use of local textiles often means the timely rescue of almost forgotten industries and artisans, some fabrics like wool have to be imported by knitwear designers to meet even limited demand. Only a brand like Bergfabel, which aims to keep alive the knowledge of traditional menswear from the Alpine region, can possibly source its most important materials from local suppliers just by remaining a modest operation. Heritage is the quest for quality, which as a reaction to decades of massproduced clothes—often using synthetics in combination with a transfer of production to cheap labor countries—has some importance beyond good taste, as it offers a better fit together with a "green" lifestyle that values local production and durability—the garment that lasts a lifetime—in contrast to the conventional seasonal cycle of fashion with its interest in continuous renewal.

Even though heritage brands have gained a strong presence in urban outfits and many pieces can be easily combined with denim and sneakers, they inevitably reconstruct lost worlds where a sense of adventure was still alive. The charm of outdoor fashion is often evoked by

From the mid-19th century on the invention of materials, machines and procedures would result in a new generation of garments offering workmen durable and reliable protection.

anonymous icons from the past: black-and-white pictures of rugged fishermen braving the open ocean, a life that has almost completely disappeared for Western men. Sometimes a slightly more personal effect is achieved by individual garments that are passed on to a next generation.

Barbour waxed coats are often acquired with the idea that they are part of the wearer's life story, while the Stutterheim raincoat is based on the model of the designer's grandfather, giving the whole enterprise a strange personal touch. The designer who has studied and recreated heritage garments with an unsurpassed eye for detail also provided this outdoor style with a more daring image than the well-mannered notion of the English countryside. Nigel Cabourn is largely fascinated by the elegant man of action, who stoically tries to plan and complete an expedition, preferably to a point on Earth where no man has stood before. But the complete surface of the world has been discovered and mapped; the era of the heroic man came to an end with Edmund Hillary and Tenzing Norgay reaching the summit of Mount Everest in 1953. Although this presents heritage outerwear with a set of strong icons, the realization of having reached natural limits also imbues the more conceptual branch of outerwear with a certain melancholic feeling.

Many menswear styles are moving in opposite directions and countrywear is no exception. A strong forward-looking tendency is active that respectfully offers an alternative to the reverence for the past by heritage labels. One strand is presented by the deconstruction of Junya Watanabe, with his 2012 spring/summer "gardener" collection offering a highly original take on countrywear basics like Wellingtons, dungarees, fishing hats, and waxed coats. This pivotal collection full of bright colors and deft patchwork can be mined for years to come. Watanabe's interest in countrywear does not stand on its own. Yosuke Aizawa also deftly deconstructs outdoors classics with his White Mountaineering label while Yuki

Matsuda offers imaginative interpretations of classic American footwear as Yuketen. Japan has always shown an interest in the work of Nigel Cabourn who even designs the Mainline collection exclusively for the country. Consequently heritage outerwear and European labels fascinated by tradition—for instance Frank Leder and Bergfabel—are easier to find in highly dedicated Japanese stores than in their own country. Some modern outerwear labels have followed Cabourn's example with The North Face exclusively presenting its Purple Label collections in Japan—the recent Detachable Lining Field Coat presenting an example of a highly innovative yet minimal take on the winter parka. The connoisseur of outdoors clothing will be rewarded by a visit to Japan where the larger cities offer a number of boutiques that not only stock the very best of the style, but often present their own interesting interpretations, too. One example is nanamica which has its own line of clothing consisting amongst others of down vests, duffle coats and a beautifully detailed soutien collar coat made of Gore-Tex.

While Europe and North America have laid the groundwork for heritage outerwear, innovative leaps could take place in Asia. South Korea in the past few years has shown a proliferation of new brands that continue to rework the countryside style. Bastong is a nonseasonal brand that focuses on the heritage ideas of using the finest materials to create garments that last. Their beautiful no. 4 waxed coat is a prime example of made-in-Korea craftsmanship, combining local, Japanese, and British materials. The influence of Barbour and Nigel Cabourn is still undeniable although one senses that the style is ready for further evolution now that the conceptual foundation of heritage clothing has been anchored. A larger scale introduction of the Asian interpretation in the West should yield positive results, as the first wave of collaborations between Western and Eastern labels seems to suggest. Besides, an ever-increasing interest in ecology and the proliferation of garden cities should result in a new outdoors lifestyle offering protection from a different combination of elements than the past.

FRANK LEDER

Berlin-based Frank Leder is without a doubt the most German of designers. For over a decade he has presented an authentic fantasy in the form of high-quality garments that are obviously inspired by the country's past but are made with a modern fit. His work exhibits a strong element of storytelling which echoes the work of British designer Nigel Cabourn, although some important differences can be observed. Leder's clothes could be described as romantic outerwear. Collections are mainly inspired by the workwear of traditional professions like butchers, woodworkers, distillers, and botanists, but also outsiders like poachers and vagabonds. These recall closed-off or hidden worlds, mostly part of the countryside—the Hinterland in German—inhabited by highly individual and often lonely men. For his 2011 fall/winter collection (and the spring/summer follow-up), Leder tried to invoke a vision of Galizien (Galicia or Halychyna), an historical area covering parts of Poland, Hungary, Ukraine, and Austria. The landscape, lost in the many transformations of the 20th century, suggests a typical Frank Leder world which only survives in stories, books, and postcards, to be reconstructed through the synthesis of fantasy and fabric.

According to the designer, the level of meaning created by stories is an integral part of menswear since the interests of men on a material level are fairly low-key. The stories create a sense of wonder, which is then enforced by the detail and quality of the fabric. The fabrics are very much part of the story as they are mostly sourced in Germany, with some—like Deutschleder—turning into a signature. Leder is fascinated by the endurance of traditional fabrics and for the most part eschews the use of synthetics, instead opting for high quality wool, linen, and cotton. Unsurprisingly his garments do not display any form of outward branding although as a substitute Leder tries to use vintage buttons made of paper or horn. There is also a humorous almost artful side to the tailoring process with Leder using German beer or red wine to dye fabrics. When given a chance garments are presented in original ways, the beer-dyed clothes, for instance, were packaged in a traditional beer mug and limited edition shirts have been baked in bread.

Interestingly enough Frank Leder clothing is hard to find in Germany, which perhaps enforces one of the points the designer likes to make, namely that local objects and customs almost become invisible through familiarity. The peculiarity of the customs has a bigger impact outside its surroundings. Next to an appreciation of quality and detail this perhaps forms

one of the reasons that Frank Leder menswear is mostly sold in Japan. Although the idea that locals interested in his garments can only reach the tailor in person surely possesses an old-fashioned charm for Leder.

To somewhat counterbalance this situation the brand has introduced a line of grooming products under the name Tradition. Usually a line of cosmetics is launched to supplement funds for the cost of collections. In the case of Tradition it has become a way to spread the concept of Frank Leder to a new audience. These tonics, soaps, bath oils, and tinctures are based on the characters Leder has explored in his menswear collections. So the Kornbrand muscle tonic is inspired by the customs of the traveling carpenter called the Zimmerman, who according to tradition has to bury a bottle of Schnapps before going on the road. All handmade products are presented in medicinal bottles with Bakelite caps which give them a vintage, collectable air.

Taken out of the narrative, Frank Leder pieces are wearable interpretations of classic menswear. So the recent Schub collection based on the crews of barges consists of pants, jackets, and shirts that can be easily combined with garments from other designers without standing out. Only the connoisseur will notice the difference by certain details and cuts. The past can be entered by choice.

INIS MEÁIN

Fashion is full of strange success stories, but one of the most surprising triumphs of recent times has undoubtedly been the rise of Irish knitwear brand Inis Meáin. The company is located on Inis Meáin (Inishmaan), the middle of the three Aran Islands that lie off the west coast of Ireland with a small population of nearly 200 people who still speak Irish. Traditionally this desolate but green island with notoriously harsh winters was inhabited by fishermen who pushed themselves into the Atlantic Ocean on curachs (narrow boats that resemble canoes, as can be seen on the brand's logo.) The hand-knitted woolen sweaters these men wore to protect themselves from the elements form the basis of the Inis Meáin collection.

The Inis Meáin Knitting Company was founded in 1976 by Tarlach de Blacam. It was mainly intended as an employment scheme for the local population while preserving one of its most characteristic products. In the early years, the handmade knits were targeted at tourists and the Irish-American community. At the end of the decade, the economic crisis demanded a radical change of strategy. As the brand would never be able to compete with low prices, it invested in knitting machines and started to focus on the high-end knitwear market. The shift paid off as the popularity of heritage, craftsmanship, and limited edition garments has grown in the past few years, eventually turning Inis Meáin into one of the world's premium knitwear brands.

Some of the knitters who still finish the sweaters by hand have been with the company from the very beginning. This ensures a certain standard and an extensive knowledge of patterns. Traditionally wool was used from local sheep but growing popularity and the disappearance of yarn spinners forced the export of high-quality blends like wool/cashmere and baby alpaca/silk from Italy and Peru.

Traditionally the fisherman sweater is fairly minimal using only a few colors (natural, black, and imported indigo.) Over the centuries families developed their own patterns to embellish the top half of knits, sometimes for luck and often inspired by the landscape or the waves of the sea. The survival of these patterns in combination with modern dyes allows Inis Meáin to constantly evolve, using tradition without being enslaved by it.

Another source of inspiration comes from celebratory knits. These garments were made for Sundays and special occasions with the richly patterned white sweater being a popular choice for First Communion. Every annual collection finds inspiration in the rich history and landscape of the island. The 2011 Máirtín Beag for instance was named after the fisherman who used to wear his sweater in this style. Starting with the fall/winter collection of 2014, the brand began to incorporate new patterns inspired by the claíochaí, ancient stone walls that can be found all over the island. The moss on the limestone is mirrored in the contrasting wool blend with yellow veins, giving the knit a unique appearance.

The company enjoys its secluded geographical position, which ensures independence and a peculiar timeframe, while limited transportation to the mainland makes rapid expansion almost impossible. Instead small adjustments are introduced while a number of models, like the Boatbuilder sweater, Floating Moss Gansey, and Classic Aran Crew, are now mainstays of the collection. Because of the almost natural, imposed limit on growth, a small number of opportunities for collaboration (with for example Yohji Yamamoto) have been seized to open new inroads into the market. A logical collaboration was initiated with English legacy brand Private White V.C. famous for its handmade garments. Using Inis Meáin's patterns with new blends and colors like the fairly unorthodox bright orange, the collaboration was quickly repeated. The past few years have also seen the brand carefully try out new styles and materials like cardigans and linen jackets which look toward a future beyond the rugged outerwear of the sea.

AIGLE

During our childhood, most of us grow accustomed to rubber boots. The practical, durable, and affordable footwear has protected generations from rainy weather and stepping into puddles. Eventually we outgrow the boots and they are relegated to practical use by farmers and outdoor enthusiasts. But the rubber boot, for a long time considered unfashionable, has slowly moved into the limelight. With the growing stylization of outerwear it was just a matter of time before the rubber boot would make something of a comeback. The originators of the boot—a French company named Aigle—seemed due for reappraisal.

Aigle was established in 1853 by American Hiram Hutchinson, the name—"eagle" in French—and logo of the brand are a reference to its American roots. A few years before, Hutchinson had met Charles Goodyear,

the inventor of the vulcanization process. With this process natural rubber could be converted into a more durable material while retaining properties like flexibility, water resistance, and shock-absorbance. Hutchinson realized the possibilities for footwear and his work-wear boots became an immediate success. During the 20th century the brand expanded with a clothing line and introduced a number of rubber boots targeted at specific outdoor pursuits like hunting.

Aigle boots are still handmade at the plant in Ingrandes, France. The half-length Bison was introduced in 1968 as a garden boot and has since grown into an all-round icon, thanks also

to the distinctive leather puller. Although most boots at first sight seem to be fit for many purposes they do possess certain characteristics which make them practical for specialist activities like fishing, hunting, and horseback riding. The sailing boots with their typical blue-and-white color scheme, for instance, have a flat sole which is optimized for stability and grip on wet boat decks. Many models have a premium version called ISO which offers extra protection. For example the Skye ISO features a thick neoprene lining which ensures extra insulation. Thanks to an eye for detail and clever reinforcements Aigle today is market leader in different categories like horseback riding (the Ecuyer), sailing (the complete range of nautical boots), and hunting (the Parcours).

The expertise in rubber makes for a logical translation to rainwear. Surprisingly enough, rubber is hardly featured in the extensive clothing line which consists of all menswear basics like polos, pants, and sneakers. The standard raincoat at first looks unassuming in the style of the classic Mackintosh but hides a removable vest for extra insulation during autumn storms. Other coats have a casual

appeal with a number of jackets featuring Gore-Tex for a breathable and waterproof solution.

Since Aigle can be considered one of the oldest operating heritage brands it has recently attracted the interest for some fruitful collaborations. The 2013 partnership with Parisian Maison Kitsuné resulted in a pair of highly coveted items, a poncho and a beautiful pair of marine boots, with rainy music festivals in mind. Another adventurous French connection was produced with underwear brand Le Slip Français in the form of a complete beachwear collection featuring a pair of rubber boots in the popular nautical style. Arguably the most prestigious collaboration was initiated in 2014 when Aigle's artistic director Gideon Day found common ground with outerwear classicist Nigel Cabourn. The fall/winter capsule collection, manufactured by Aigle following Cabourn concepts, turned into an interesting synthesis of British and French fabrics, of workwear and outdoors styles. Of course a boot was presented—Le Godiot—that mixes rubber with leather for a robust interpretation of the

vintage worker's boot. But undoubtedly the most beautiful piece is the La Bricard parka which perfectly symbolizes the co-operation with an outer shell from Halley Stevenson navy-blue wax cotton and an orange removable inner duck-down jacket made from French nylon.

GRENSON

The use of the brogue shoe has undergone a fascinating evolution. Nowadays the more conservative interpretations are considered perfectly acceptable as business shoe. Although it is hard to imagine, the brogue was first worn as an outerwear shoe in parts of Ireland and Scotland. The rough leather of the shoe was enhanced with decorative perforations, which allowed for the more efficient drainage of moisture when walking through wet terrains. The perforations eventually spread to other types of shoe like the Derby, Oxford, or leather boot, often resulting in ornate patterns and contrasting colors. The working-class shoe became a countrywear staple and even crossed over into womenswear. English shoemaker Grenson offers many types of brogues, with some shoes like the Stanley having changed very little in over 80 years, although alternative models use suede or rubber soles instead of classic leather. The Fred, a triple-welted brogue boot, combines style and comfort for a unique countrywear shoe.

GUDRUN & GUDRUN

The scarf is one of humanity's oldest garments. It can be worn in different ways and has a practical use for keeping the neck area warm, especially when wearing a formal coat. The garment also has a strong symbolic function; in Great Britain, for example, the academic scarf with colored stripes represents different colleges. Scarves can be made from a number of materials like wool, cashmere, and linen. The thin woven scarf became a popular menswear staple at the beginning of the 21st century often worn in combination with a T-shirt. Knitwear specialists Guðrun & Guðrun, based on the Faroe Islands, make some of the most comfortable scarves using different blends of mohair, baby alpaca, and wool. The thick luxurious scarves will keep the wearer warm while their rustic style will give every outfit that something extra. Their Gisleyg, mainly made of mohair, is perhaps their most conventional scarf, which can be found in different colors and will protect the wearer during many a winter storm.

HOLLAND & HOLLAND

Tweed is a woolen fabric that is closely woven in a herringbone or check pattern. The material is a staple of British outerwear since its durability and resistance to moisture perfectly suit the climate. The tweed jacket became a popular upper-class garment for hunting and is still associated with countryside elites. No wonder that gunmaker Holland & Holland features tweed jackets in its clothing collection. Holland & Holland was founded in 1835 and is highly regarded as a manufacturer of the finest handmade shotguns. As part of their small collection they offer a hand-cut tweed jacket with an exclusive design of moss with burgundy lines and lining. The Half Norfolk shooting jacket features three buttons, larger pockets, storm cuffs, and pivot sleeves for better movement when raising one's arms. The tweed has a Nanobloc finish which offers protection against showers and stains. The Signature shooting jacket comes in a toffee-colored check based on the design of the founder's jacket.

HUNTER

The discovery of vulcanization immediately found its application in rubber boots. Two Americans established a company in Edinburgh for the production of, among other things, footwear using the new waterproof and resilient material. The North Rubber Company, which would eventually be named Hunter Boot, produced a vast number of boots during both World Wars, which also meant that "Wellies" became a household name. The green rubberWellington boot introduced in 1955 offered perfect yet stylish protection against mud and became a countryside standard. The original Wellington boot with the characteristic buckle and heel still is Hunter's best selling item, especially after being presented in fashionable colors. Over the years many technical versions, like the Balmoral or the snow boot, have been introduced which offer improved insulation and protection for use on different terrains. Hunter wellies are handmade from 28 parts and available in the classic tall length and a shorter version.

BARBOUR

Barbour is one of the quintessential British clothing brands. As one of the touchstones of heritage clothing the influence of Barbour has grown enormously in the past few years. J. Barbour & Sons Ltd.—the official name of the company—was founded in 1894 by John Barbour. The company in the coast town of South Shields established itself as an importer of oilcloth, a waterproof material made of linen or cotton cloth with a coating of boiled linseed oil. This fabric would play a crucial role in the development of Barbour. The first Barbour jackets were designed for local fishermen, who still used primitive protection against foul weather, and industrial workers in the north-east region of England. The functional jackets quickly mutated into different types like the trench coat, cape, and riding coat. Early on, the collar was made of a distinctive fabric, for instance, velvet, which differed from the outer shell and lining, eventually morphing into corduroy which turned into one of the distinctive marks of the Barbour jacket.

Barbour anticipated many trends we now take for granted, like clothing for different lifestyles or the influence of military apparel on everyday fashion. Through the years the appeal of the jackets outgrew the functionalism for workmen to become the outdoors classic that oozes British style. The jacket is made for the British climate and its many outdoors activities like hiking, fishing, wildfowling, and hunting. To this was added a motorcycle line in 1936 thanks to the personal interest of Duncan Barbour in motorbike riding. The separate line was christened Barbour International, which would dominate the sport for decades to come. Barbour International also attracted the attention of an American icon in the form of stylish actor Steve McQueen who, as part of the American motorcycle team competing in the International Six Day trials, purchased their racing suits in 1964. Recently McQueen was honored with a special capsule line and in 2013 a shop catering exclusively to the expanding Barbour International brand was opened in Piccadilly, London.

For awhile Barbour suffered from an archaic image but a surprising comeback has seen the label diversify beyond its famous jackets with collections of knitwear, shirts, trousers, polos, and footwear. Although it is still considered to be the prime brand for life in the English countryside Barbour's newfound popularity is often related to its growing use in urban outfits. The brand now features four main lines (International, Lifestyle, Heritage, and Sporting) which offer thematic collections and collaborations, for instance, with the Japanese brand White Mountaineering and a range of

stunning limited editions with Soto Berlin. Many collections delve into the rich archive for inspiration, resulting in modern updates of forgotten pieces. Nevertheless, the wax jackets continue to be the most popular pieces, especially those collected under the Barbour Originals moniker: the Bedale, Border, Northumbria, and Beaufort. These jackets—often constructed from up to 160 parts—are still assembled in the South Shields factory. The Beaufort remains the brand's largest seller. The jacket

was first sold in 1983 as a stylish up-date of the shooting jacket and features all the famous Barbour details like the corduroy collar which can be turned into a storm fly, a detachable hood, deep pockets, two-way ring zipper, and tartan lining.

People are known to attach themselves to Barbour wax coats, claiming they have a lived-in feeling and gain character over the years. Coats often last a lifetime and are passed on to the next wearer. Aware of this personal appeal Barbour offers a repair service which addresses different types of wear and damage. The South Shields factory alone process 14,000 coats a year, often turning them into a unique piece. No wonder that for many people Barbour has become a synonym for the waxed jacket.

THE WAXED JACKET

The waxed jacket is a classic countryside rain-coat. The outer fabric is made of linen or cotton cloth with an added layer of wax that turns it into waterproof material. English manufacturer Barbour has been associated with the waxed jacket since its launch in 1894. Throughout the years, the company has added details, like the corduroy collar and tartan lining, which have become generic. Thanks to its unassuming use of colors, sturdiness, and effective protection from British weather, the Barbour grew into an icon of country life. Nowadays Barbour presents a large number of waxed coats in different lengths and styles. Both military chic and the motor jacket have left their marks on the collection often resulting in a more modern silhouette. Nonetheless, the classic waxed jackets, especially the Beaufort, remain the brand's biggest sellers. These jackets are still manufactured in England and feature a number of details which make the Barbour waxed coat into a garment that lasts a lifetime.

SCOTT-NICHOL

Socks are perhaps the most underrated menswear item. The eye-catching shoe receives all the attention but without the humble sock, most shoes would be uncomfortable. While in formal wear socks are expected to match the color of the pants, one is allowed a greater degree of freedom in countrywear. Here the focus lies on warmth and moisture control during colder seasons while comfort has a high priority when walking over large distances. Scott-Nichol, the quintessential country-sock maker, which has been producing its garments for over 70 years, is still based in England. Their socks are made of cotton or wool blends, occasionally featuring an added touch of silk or cashmere for extra softness. Since informal circumstances allow for a more personal touch, Scott-Nichol socks offer a host of eccentric patterns and colorful combinations, which immediately brighten any countryside outfit. With its strong English roots, Scott-Nichol also offers striped socks which give a nod to rugby and college life.

STUTTERHEIM

In Northern countries a raincoat is indispensable. Swedish company Stutterheim is a newcomer in outerwear with its rubber raincoat quickly turning into a modern classic. The garment is the brainchild of Alexander Stutterheim who one day discovered his grandfather's raincoat and was struck by its style. Eventually he constructed a replica with a slightly updated fit which became a runaway success. The original Stutterheim raincoat called Arholma is made of thick rubberized cotton with a cotton lining. The coat is hand stitched while the seams are carefully closed off with tape. The style is minimal with a silhouette that harkens back to the 1960s. A slightly simpler version was introduced under the name Stockholm and features just the outer shell with double-welded seams. The raincoat was available at first in black but over the years more colors have been introduced along with upbeat striped versions. A 25-centimeter longer Stockholm is also available ensuring complete body protection.

LOCK & CO.

The flat cap, also known as a bonnet, probably has been a part of the male wardrobe for centuries. The headgear is rounded with a stiff front and comes in different styles. The flat cap reached the height of its popularity as an all-round hat in the 19th century and beginning of the 20th century. Many of the alternative names for the cap, like driving cap, cycling cap or golf cap, reveal its versatility. The flat cap can be made of leather, corduroy, cotton, and wool, although the most common material is tweed, which ensures durability and some protection from rain. Nowadays, the flat cap is considered old-fashioned although from time to time an adventurous man will combine the cap with a modern outfit. James Lock & Co. established in 1676 is one of the oldest family companies still in operation. The London shop is specialized in hats and still makes the best tweed flat caps by hand. The flat cap comes in different models like the Gill, Turnberry, Sandwich, and Bentley with ample choice in patterns.

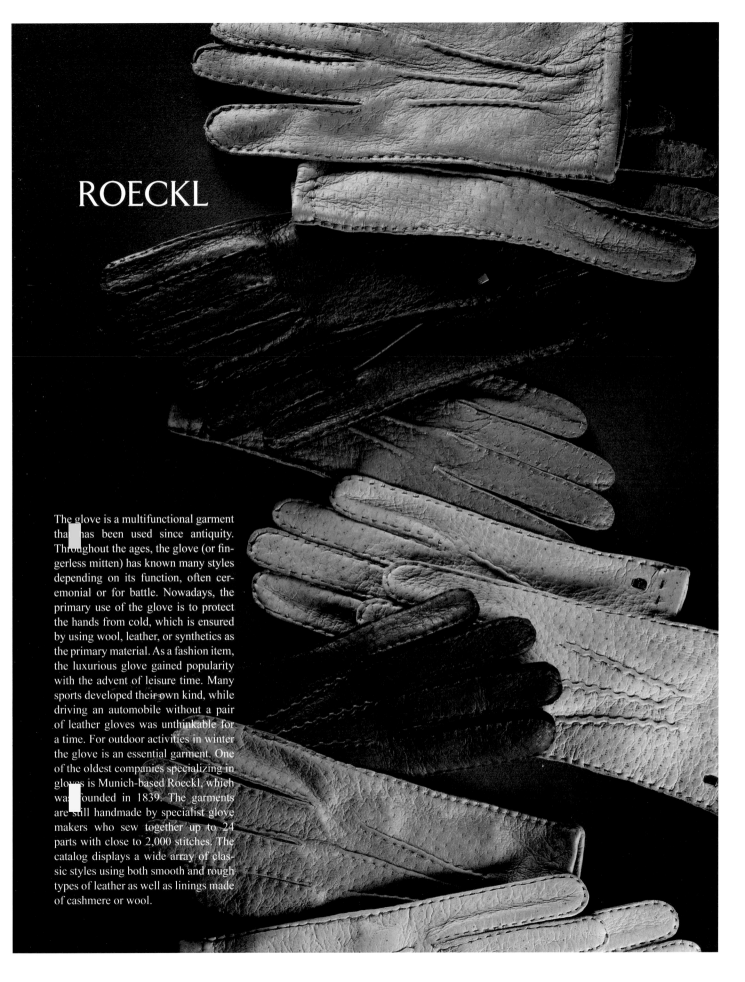

ROECKL

The glove is a multifunctional garment that has been used since antiquity. Throughout the ages, the glove (or fingerless mitten) has known many styles depending on its function, often ceremonial or for battle. Nowadays, the primary use of the glove is to protect the hands from cold, which is ensured by using wool, leather, or synthetics as the primary material. As a fashion item, the luxurious glove gained popularity with the advent of leisure time. Many sports developed their own kind, while driving an automobile without a pair of leather gloves was unthinkable for a time. For outdoor activities in winter the glove is an essential garment. One of the oldest companies specializing in gloves is Munich-based Roeckl, which was founded in 1839. The garments are still handmade by specialist glove makers who sew together up to 24 parts with close to 2,000 stitches. The catalog displays a wide array of classic styles using both smooth and rough types of leather as well as linings made of cashmere or wool.

WOLFEN

The knit sweater is a basic element of every man's winter wardrobe. After a period of industrial production using synthetic blends, the artisanal knit sweater has made a triumphant comeback with a number of local brands offering knit-wear made from high-quality wool. These are garments that will not only keep you warm but also last a lifetime, while possessing a timeless quality. One of Europe's best-kept secrets when it comes to knitwear is the Berlin-based brand Wolfen. The label was started in 2001 by Jacqueline Huste and named after her birthplace. Wolfen specializes in limited edition knits that are knitted by hand using merino wool or cotton. These are unassuming but beautiful sweaters that never follow trends. In contrast to many competitors Wolfen knits are soft and thin while retaining their insulating quality. A small selection can be ordered in their online shop, while the complete collection is only available in the Auguststrasse boutique at surprisingly affordable prices.

YUKETEN

Walking forms an essential part of the countryside lifestyle, which makes the leather boot the most important outerwear garment. A good leather boot should offer support and comfort while protecting feet from moisture. Most boots have rubber soles for durability and protection. Since 1989 Yuketen has offered an original take on the leather boot. Designer Yuki Matsuda is mainly inspired by American footwear classics. Yuketen boots are mostly handmade in the United States with the use of a traditional sewing technique. While the brand offers some round-nosed boots like the Johnson and Duck boot, it is mostly celebrated for the signature Maine Guide boot. The moccasin-style boot was inspired by wilderness guides from the 1940s and has known countless interpretations over the years. The sole is made of eight layers of rubber with a leather underfoot. Steel reinforcement helps to redistribute weight resulting in less fatigue, while the leather insoles will take on the shape of the wearer's feet.

FORMAL

FORMAL ATTIRE

OFF THE CUFF

DESPITE ALL OF THE SOCIAL PRESSURES ASSOCIATED
WITH FORMAL ATTIRE, THIS STYLE OF DRESS HAS ALWAYS BEEN
AN EXPRESSION OF PERSONALITY. A SUIT AND HAT NO LONGER
ONLY REFLECT PAST STYLES, BUT ARE RATHER INCREASINGLY
SIGNS OF FASHION-FORWARD COOLNESS.

by

JOSH SIMS

For many men, the idea of formal attire—suit, dress shirt, tie—can fill them with dread. This is, perhaps, a modern phenomenon. Once, every man wore some version of formal dress and men of the professional classes or above would wear it every day. All clothes were tailored and the suit, as it's commonly conceived, was the bedrock of male dress; no man would dream of wearing a suit without a tie, which in turn necessitated a stiff-collared shirt—a garment that until the early part of the 20th century was still regarded as underwear, to be hidden away under one's tailoring. Likewise, no man would dream of leaving the house without wearing a hat. To do so could mark one out as a social outcast. In Dickens' *Great Expectations,* Pip notices that the convict Magwitch was "a man with no hat." This was not good.

But for the latter half of the same century at least, such dress—now competing with casual clothing—marked one out more as a cog in some corporate machine, as a "salaryman," as the Japanese still call them. Unless one was attending an event at which formal dress was then (though less so now) traditionally expected—a wedding or a funeral, for example, at which the wearing of formal clothes was a mark of respect—a

> **The suit, has come to signify a new "cool," rather than the old "square."**

suit and tie were put on begrudgingly. Yes, such a uniform meant little thought was needed when getting dressed for work in the morning. But it was also another indication of the power of employer over employee, of the need to follow rules laid down by others. The wearing of formal clothing was rarely a pleasure.

Indeed, over the early post-war decades—when casual dressing first took hold in menswear—some elements of formal dress came to be perceived as so outmoded or even oppressive—literally hemming a man in—that they were rejected altogether, regardless of seeming social pressures. The bow tie, suspenders, the three-piece suit—all fell from favor, returning only occasionally as fashion might encourage. The formal hat all but disappeared entirely: in a world of increased car travel and central heating, who needed a hat? US President John F. Kennedy refused outright to wear one, winning him the nickname "Hatless Jack," but in doing so brought the American hat industry to its knees. Kennedy associated a formal hat with the style of older generations—by not wearing one he came to look youthful, like the first "modern" president, which played well in polls.

Thankfully, this negativity towards formal dressing has changed in recent years with casual style becoming much more dominant in menswear—this has meant that formal attire can be worn again as a matter more of choice than of necessity. Dressing up can once again be fun. With it has come a revival of interest in the craft of bespoke tailoring from the likes of London's Savile Row and New York's Madison Avenue, for example. The fashion industry has embraced more directional styling for the suit too—skinny lapels, ankle-skimming trousers or a more shrunken fit, for example—or has revived period aesthetics the likes of the 1930s wide peak lapels and three-piece suiting. The suit, in short, has come to signify a new "cool," rather than the old "square." Hats are no longer the preserve of fancy dress costumes.

Indeed, if formal dressing was once so rule-bound as to give most men the impression that it left little room for self-expression, that is no longer the case, even if some rules are there for good reason—never wear novelty socks, never wear a ready-made bow tie, never do up all the front buttons on your suit, never wear sneakers with a suit—and even if it has meant men learning a new appreciation for the dapper accessory.

Look, perhaps, to the Italians for inspiration. When Baldessare Castiglione wrote The Book of the Courtier in 1528, he posited what he called the "universal rule in all human affairs"—sprezzatura, a facade of nonchalance that concealed the artistry required to pull off challenges with aplomb, regarded even at the time as both romantic and deceptive in almost equal measure. It was, in effect, the original conception of cool. This developed into the idea—deeply embedded in Italian culture—of "la bella figura," a system of etiquette through clothing, a way of adding to the beauty and order of the world through one's choice of suiting cloth, collar or cuff, and something of a performance of one's place in the world. Formal attire is merely the canvas on which one artfully drapes a cashmere scarf, or undoes one's cuff buttons to show off some tasteful cufflinks.

History, certainly, has shaped the modern idea of the suit, responding mostly to practical necessity—a surprise to those who think of the suit as embodying the very opposite. The 17th-century English king Charles II took to wearing the basis of the suit—a jacket, waistcoat, and breeches, the forerunner of pants—and, since the royal coffers were low and frugality in order, encouraged the wearing of these "suits" in dark silks. It was Charles who also introduced the idea of a suit for men buttoning right to left—this allowed the right-handed man to fasten or unfasten his jacket while leaving his right hand free to draw a sword. These days, it might be to draw a smartphone. The following century, the suit was adapted to make riding easier, especially for cavalrymen—the jacket being shortened, cut away at the front, made more form-fitting and in wool (so as to be warmer), with the wearer's habit of turning back the collar being the beginnings of the lapel. The suit as it is known today is, in effect, an ancestor of military equestrian clothing.

More surprisingly, even that seemingly most useless of garments, the tie, also begins its life in the military. Croatian mercenaries for the French army during the Thirty Years' War (1618–48) wore a cravat-like tie—"cravat" possibly being a linguistic mangling of "Croat"—ostensibly as a means of signaling their comradeship. It took King Louis XIV

If once formal dressing was so rule-bound as to give most men the impression that it left little room for self-expression, that is no longer the case.

to adopt the style and give it credibility in civilian society. It was from here that a simple scarf, one perhaps in flax and trimmed in lace, began its evolution: from a garment that was initially wrapped around the neck many times, leaving just short ends on show, to silk neckbands knotted in a bow, and finally the variation in which the cloth was knotted to leave the ends long.

But from the outset how one knotted one's tie—perhaps chosen from the many types of knots that would become fashionable—became an all-important statement of individuality. Louis—as king, a man used to being physically dressed by menservants—is said to have insisted on knotting his own neckwear from the selection presented to him. George "Beau" Brummell, the hugely influential 18th-century English dandy, would repeatedly attempt to knot his tie just so, working through a pile of freshly laundered and starched linens then worn as ties until he was properly satisfied. As the *Journal des Dames* noted in 1835, "La cravate, c'est l'homme." Come the 20th century, and the way a pocket square was folded into one's pocket—straight and neat, or like a range of mountain peaks—would win the same attention.

The *Journal des Dames* noted in 1835, "La cravate, c'est l'homme."

Indeed, there is a lesson in this: that through the course of the history of formal dressing, men of imagination have always sought to remain individuals, no matter how regimented acceptable formal dress became. Arguably, the idea that formal dressing meant wearing an indistinct uniform was never really the case—even our style icons have often lived in times in which formal attire was the norm, but have stood out nevertheless. In his professional life, Fred Astaire, for example, was associated with the most formal style of dress of all—top hat, white tie, and tails, a style perhaps only now seen in old movies. In his private life, he was typically

well tailored too. He insisted that his suits be subtle and once said, "I just don't like a suit to stand out. I don't want someone looking twice at me and saying in an incredulous tone, 'what was that?'"

But he chose his suits with extreme attention to detail—he typically took his suits back to the tailors at least six times to have adjustments made—and accessorized them in a way that still allowed him to stand out. He would wear a gold pin to hold his shirt together at the desired break; he might wear brown suede or white buckskin Oxford shoes with no regard for supposed rules of coordinating them with socks or pants; he would wear a belt with the buckle pushed to one side or, more distinctively, would hold his trousers up by use of a silk scarf or tie. As for that pocket square, he would simply shove it into his breast pocket so it blossomed out like a bouquet.

Similarly, the industrialist and head of the Fiat car giant family Gianni Agnelli was, by virtue of his line of work, typically expected to wear business attire. This, of course, was immaculate: as the man who at one point controlled 4.4 percent of Italy's entire GDP, he could afford the finest bespoke tailoring. But it was how he wore it that would see him acclaimed as one of the century's most stylish men. A fan of double-breasted suits, he would occasionally wear these undone, a look that went against supposed dress propriety; he would wear his tie—typically tied using an Italian four-in-hand knot, wrapped twice rather than once around—just a little undone, and a little off-center; said tie might also be worn with the narrow end longer than the blade, again considered a faux pas; a fan of button-down collared shirts, he would wear his collars unbuttoned, whether wearing a tie or not; and he wore his watch strapped on over his dress shirt's cuff, not under it.

Agnelli said that he was so busy he simply didn't have the time to pull back his cuff whenever he needed to look at his watch. That might be true. But it is more tempting to believe that he knew it looked right as a reflection of his personality. Formally dressed he may have been. A mere "suit" he was not.

RICHARD JAMES

Richard James might be called a kind of revolutionary. Back in 1992, suits were either cheap or, if you shopped on London's Savile Row, rather expensive. Neither end of the market had much concern for contemporary style, being stuck in a rut of conservatism. James, a former buyer for seminal London boutique Browns, and his business partner Sean Dixon, changed that—helping to give back to "The Row" the cool it had during the 1960s when the likes of Tommy Nutter, tailoring iconoclast and James's sartorial forebear, had managed to make tailoring interesting to the jet set.

James took a £10,000 loan and, thanks to a bargain deal on a condemned Savile Row shop, introduced a fresh perspective on tailoring: not baggy and deconstructed like the Italian and Japanese designers of the era were offering, nor traditional and stuffy. This was stripped-back,

fuss-free, slim, sharp tailoring for a new generation to whom good tailoring was something alien, even unappealing. Some of the canvases and interlining found in more traditional tailoring, which provided its stiffness, were abandoned; the one- or two-button single-breasted suits with a slightly longer, more waisted jacket with deep side vents became his signature, as did James's experimentation with color, fabric, and pattern. It was James who created a camouflage suit—initially, he has said, "for a customer who likes the opera, but doesn't like wearing suits—it got the reaction he wanted"—that would be worn by Robert de Niro and Dustin Hoffman in 1997 for a George magazine cover. A bright purple, one-button velvet suit might be considered characteristically James.

Unlike tailoring of the time, James, he said, appealed to a

certain attitude—confident, vibrant, progressive—rather than a certain age. It was James, after all, who was the

first bespoke tailor to advertise in the fashion press, the first to make a TV advertisement—it showed a man dressing himself in Richard James before jumping to his death from a high-rise building. "Richard James: menswear for every occasion," as the caption for the controversial or tongue-in-cheek ad had it. He spread his name through a series of sometimes off-beat collaborations—with football strip makers Umbro and Condor Cycles, but also with SpongeBob SquarePants. The likes of Elton John and Gianni Versace became regular Richard James customers, with David Beckham, Tom Cruise, Bryan Ferry, and Michael Douglas among the many following. Mick Jagger and Paul McCartney, both of whom had been tailored by

Tommy Nutter, were now tailored by Richard James.

"The 1980s were all about labels. It was considered a huge compliment if someone said to you 'is that Comme?' We were finding that when customers wore one of our suits people would come up to them and say 'you look good,'" James once noted. With English tailoring, "While you should respect the past, you have to push forward." James, thinking like a contemporary brand, was also quick to expand into shirts, knitwear, shoes made in Northampton (with its historic reputation for making the world's best men's footwear), and other menswear essentials, especially accessories, like ties, pocket squares, and socks, that gave him freer rein to explore color.

The old guard of Savile Row may not have been entirely impressed by James's arrival: "Parasites who don't know one end of a needle from the other," was one putdown. But, as James once said, "Savile Row was seemingly a place catering for older gentleman, and didn't have anything youthful about it. We respected the street totally but just wanted to do tailoring in a modern way. Now we've somehow become part of the establishment." Or, perhaps, even created their own. Many other young tailors have followed the path he and Dixon pioneered, helping to make what came to be dubbed British tailoring's "New Establishment."

TURNBULL & ASSER

Spot some foxing on a man's shirt collar—that fraying along the edges consistent with repeated wear over many years—and, in times of short shelf lives and disposability, it might be tempting to ask why he doesn't buy another shirt. But then maybe it is a Turnbull & Asser—built to last.

Indeed, having evolved its manufacturing process over a century, during which time it has fostered generations of expert shirt-makers—apprenticed for five years, allowed to work on bespoke only after ten—and developed a pedigree for its made-in-England products, Turnbull & Asser might well claim to know its business rather well. Let some 13 people apply that know-how to the 25 steps required to make one of the company's shirts, and some five hours later the result is clear in the finishing, fit, and finesse. And, if you wait long enough, even in the foxing.

A closer look at the details of a Turnbull & Asser dress shirt, however, might be more convincing than lots of numbers. There is, for example, the single-needle stitching throughout, for both its fine finish and its strength. There is the gusset, which reinforces the side seams. The buttons, which are cut from the deepest part of mother-of-pearl shell, and affixed with a cross-lock

stitch, so one won't unravel in your hand as you're dressing late for a meeting. The two-ply, 120-thread count cloths, woven in Italy, are exclusive. The collar—something of a signature—is made with a floating, rather than fused, bias cut interlining to ensure it stays down, the edge gently curved to ensure it sits well. And, to return to numbers, while shirt buffs like to talk of a two-part or split yoke, a Turnbull & Asser yoke is made of four parts, to give flexibility across the upper back.

Certainly, what is rarer still is to find all this on a ready-to-wear shirt—indeed, Turnbull & Asser, which has stood for more than a century has stood preeminently on London's Jermyn Street. Known as the world Mecca for top-end shirt-makers, it has borrowed many of its construction detailing from its bespoke service, which in turn has had to raise the ante. There, for example, one will find that the fabric for sleeve and chest has been painstakingly matched. And that, if after perhaps decades of wear that foxing is starting to look a little too bohemian, both collar and cuffs can be replaced.

Turnbull & Asser's is a distinctive style too thanks to its traditional use of bold color and pattern, right from its founding in 1885 by John Turnbull and Ernest

Asser—and not least because each design was hand-painted onto card before being interpreted by the weavers. That meant strong lines and graphic simplicity—two inch-wide stripes, polka dots with checks, as well as striking combinations of the primaries—all of which provided interest under a conservative three-piece suit, which would have been standard, everyday wear for many of its customers.

Certainly, historically Turnbull & Asser's bolder creations helped shape not only the "peacock revolution" of the 1960s—when menswear found its own voice away from the strictures of sober suiting—but also took their inspiration from characters in the many seminal films the shirt-maker has outfitted, from Omar Sharif in *Dr. Zhivago* (1965) to Robert Redford in *The Great Gatsby* (1974) and Sean Connery in *Dr. No* (1962). Bond creator Ian Fleming also bought his shirts there. And as in fiction, so in fact—Turnbull & Asser's was the shirt of choice for fashion influencers the likes of Andy Warhol, Roy Halston, Hardy Amies, and Ralph Lauren, as well as historic figures from Pablo Picasso to Ronald Reagan and Winston Churchill. Such was the appeal of the cut and color of Turnbull & Asser shirts that celebrated women such as Katharine Hepburn and Lauren Bacall also wore them.

ISAAC REINA

Perhaps he thinks of his bags as small pieces of architecture—after all, Isaac Reina studied architecture at university in his native Barcelona. "It's an influence for me—in terms of geometry and proportions and volumes," the Paris-based designer has said. Certainly his unisex leather goods—briefcases, satchels, messenger bags, document cases, card holders, tablet cases, wallets and the like, all made in France—might well be called minimalistic and monochromatic—one signature is the use of bold color, although classic black, tan, and navy also figure in his collections—with even the hardware that helps hold the pieces together hidden from view beneath the soft leather.

"To me minimalism has never gone away since its inception in 1900 by Adolf Loos and, later, by the Bauhaus. Utilitarian design looks to accomplish a primary function in a direct way—and if it succeeds an object can become legendary," Reina once noted. "Say less but in a strong way—it has more impact. The most difficult task is always to simplify"

Construction is certainly understated, making for products that are neither traditional nor so fashionable as to become quickly dated: his wallets, for example, are more pieces of industrial design than traditional leatherwork, made super-slim to fit into the tightest of back pockets, or the inside pocket of a suit jacket without ruining the line; his Ultra Soft Backpack is just that, having been made from the kind of leather usually reserved for making gloves; his document cases are paper thin, without sacrificing strength; his 014 or 48 Hours calfskin bag, a weekender, is built to lie entirely flat as an octagon when empty, making it a good bag to pack away when traveling—ideal for all the unexpected things you

come home with. This is even more the case here because Reina likes to strip away anything extraneous to the function, making his leather goods notably lightweight.

"For me this is the first idea for the bags—to make the simplest and lightest available," Reina has explained. "In classic bags they use a lot of lining and inside materials to construct and support. I wanted to get rid of that. It expresses my point of view that one should have a light life."

The emphasis in his products is furthermore on detail rather than big statements (he has said that he likes his goods to offer no "big show, [to be] not too loud") as might be expected from a designer who spent seven years as an assistant to Véronique Nichanian, the menswear designer for Hermes—he didn't apply for the job; he just sent in his CV and found himself with a job by the end of the month. But, although menswear is his background, Reina felt that accessories were his calling, setting up his own business in 2006, building it while also freelancing for Maison Martin Margiela. There the acclaimed Belgian designer encouraged him to push more toward the avant garde. He took that advice to heart.

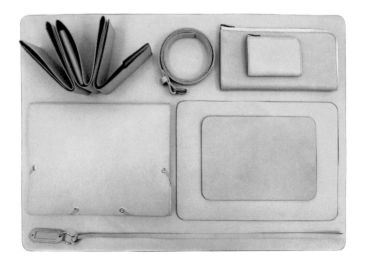

BARENA

Barena is less an Italian company than a proudly Venetian one—it takes its name from the local term *baro*, referring to the territory in the Venetian lagoon between land and water. The clothes from Barena—established by Sandro Zara in 1961—are inspired by the land and water too, taking their cue from lagunare, a certain ancient dress aesthetic of functional pieces suitable for farming, fishing, and hunting. As such, layering is a key style, with one of its key pieces being a traditional garment: the knitted vest or waistcoat. Barena, which often reproduces vintage fabrics, makes its version from wool, or a more lightweight linen/cotton blend, in dark textural shades, sometimes with barely there patterns for added interest. The result is a versatile garment, giving additional warmth and style under a jacket without having to wear a full three-piece suit.

DUCHAMP

The invention of the French or double cuff shirt by French tailors during the mid-1800s—also named in homage to Dumas' *The Count of Monte Cristo*, which sparked a craze for the cufflink—changed the way men dressed. The shirt was considered underwear, and etiquette dictated no part of it should be visible beneath your suit; new cuffs and links saw the rules of dress now dictate that two inches of cuff should be shown. Launched in 1989, cufflink designers Duchamp were also inspired by France—by the finding of a cache of vintage cufflinks in a Paris flea market. The company soon became known as a specialist maker of cufflinks in a variety of styles, both classic—silk knots and ovals, for example—and more contemporary, with signature florals, paisleys, and stripes made using materials as diverse as enamel, mother of pearl, and carbon fiber.

CROMBIE

Established in Aberdeen, Scotland in 1805, Crombie has a long history in making coats. It supplied them to the Confederate army during the American Civil War (1861–1865), the gray cloth supplied giving rise to the color coming to be known as "rebel gray" to the French during the Prussian siege of Paris in 1871. Its so-called "British Warm" coat—double-breasted, with peak lapels and epaulettes, and sometimes worn belted, from which the wrap coat later evolved—was later worn by British officers in the First World War. In civilian life, it also defined the modern over- or covert coat, with its contrasting velvet collar, ticket pocket, poacher's inside pocket, distinctive bands of reinforcing stitching at cuff and hem, created in a smooth, thorn-proof, fawn or charcoal fabric. A Crombie was favored by Sinatra, Kennedy, and Cary Grant, as well as by influential subcultures from Teddy Boys to mods, and skinheads alike.

CHRISTY'S HATS

"Men are actually re-learning why they might wear hats again—not only are they an immensely practical accessory, but they define you. We're heading toward positive times for the hat again," Steve Clark, managing director of Christy's has argued. His company, established by Miller Christy in 1773 in London where it still manufactures, and pioneer of the Panama hat, has certainly supplied formal styles during times when social mores dictated that no man, rich or poor, would leave the house without a hat. Like its main rival, Lock, which invented the bowler hat, Christy's continues to use traditional methods to make its trilby, fedora and pork pie styles, even the homburg worn by Marlon Brando in *The Godfather*, creating the felt by using steam and water to lock together animal fibers, stiffening using shellac, blocking, flanging, and finishing, all by hand.

E. TAUTZ

A scarf goes a long way to adding an element of color and individuality to attire that, necessarily conformist, might otherwise be sober and indistinct. Indeed, acquire one in lightweight Scottish cashmere, such as that by E. Tautz, and it need not be confined to winter months either; it is long enough, too to be tied in multiple ways, or wrapped around the neck repeatedly when chills set in. E. Tautz is perhaps used to designing garments with such practicality in mind—established in 1867 in London, owned by the Savile Row tailor Norton & Son since 1968, and relaunched in 2005, it has long specialized in simple, British-made clothing inspired by military and sportswear style, an approach it has maintained in the 21st century.

E. MARINELLA

"It's true that there are more occasions for men not to wear a tie but there are still those occasions when a man should wear a tie to show respect," he argues. "That might be for an important meeting or going to the theatre. Ultimately the tie isn't just about dressing up—it's a statement of respect," Maurizio Marinella has said. He is the owner of E. Marinella, the company established by his grandfather Eugenio in Naples in 1914 and widely regarded as makers of the world's best neckwear. Wearers become members of a kind of unspoken fraternity of power-players with a shared taste in fine ties. The Agnelli family—Italian industrialist owners of the Fiat Group— wore Marinella, as did the Duke of Windsor and John F. Kennedy, Chirac, Gorbachev, Clinton, Sarkozy, and Prince Charles. The ties are all handmade in Naples using English fabrics, folded seven times towards the inside part to provide a luxurious density, and lined by artisanal makers that require special training. Only four ties are ever made of any one design, so each is effectively unique to the customer.

STEPHAN SCHNEIDER

The unstructured jacket suits the modern, more relaxed business climate, giving comfort of the kind found in a cardigan, but with a hint of formality. The lack of structure, however, places additional emphasis on fabric and pattern. A designer the likes of Stephan Schneider—who has built a reputation for soft, loose, artistic but accessible menswear since graduating from the acclaimed Royal Academy of Fine Arts in Antwerp in 1994—meets these demands, known as he is to split his time between designing the textile and the silhouette of each piece. "When your textile is strong, you don't have to invent pants with three legs," as the German designer has put it. His soft-shouldered, unlined jackets—cut by hand and assembled in Belgium—might, for example, come in a dark, lightweight, textural basket weave or in a large, muted check.

ANDERSON'S

It sounds English but actually Anderson's, as specialist belt-makers, was founded by Carlo Valenti in Parma, Italy, in 1966—after six years working for another manufacturer and deciding he could improve on what the market offered (it was, however, named in Valenti's appreciation of British style, notably the Savile Row tailors Anderson and Sheppard). Over the decades, the family company has continued to manufacture in Italy and has won a reputation especially for its woven belts—weaving in premium leather, suede, cotton, various colors of elastic, as well as making more traditional unwoven leather styles. Parma has a historic reputation as a capital of leather-goods manufacture and it is from the local populace that Anderson's draws its small team of artisans to make its belts by hand. Anderson's might well now be Europe's oldest dedicated belt manufacturer—after all, it was only after the 1930s that the wearing of belts to hold up one's trousers became commonplace at all.

HACKETT

"I think we've probably romanced that English look a bit, because otherwise a plain gray suit is just a plain gray suit, with nothing to get much excited by," Jeremy Hackett, co-founder of Hackett in London in the early 1980s, admits. "Yet if that English look doesn't really exist as it's imagined then people certainly like it, extraordinarily so." It is, he adds, exemplified by the three-piece suit—jacket, pants, and waistcoat—which characterized the "city gent" of the 1950s, through to the Wall Street power-dressing "Gordon Gekko" era of the 1980s, and has since moved in and out of fashion. Hackett's is an accessible version, bridging classic and contemporary, cut slim, natural shoulder, strong chest, and in traditional English fabrics the likes of subtle pinstripes and windowpane checks, with the detailing reflecting that found in bespoke tailoring of the kind that inspired the creation of the company—initially as a market stall selling second-hand suits.

LUDWIG REITER

The brogue—with its characteristic punch-hole pattern, once punched all the way through the leather to allow Irish bog water to drain out—is a classic men's footwear style, in a slim-line style to wear with suiting, or chunkier for less dressed-up wear. A benchmark version is the Budapester brogue, with its Derby-style lacing, one of the most distinctive styles from Ludwig Reiter, Vienna's last makers of bench-made shoes, founded in 1885. The distinction of the style is that it still looks contemporary. Classic, as noted by Till Reiter, fourth-generation head of the family company, "isn't something that stays static for eternity, but which evolves through use. People used to walk a lot more, so today shoes don't have to be so sturdy. Or hard to break in—it can be difficult to explain to someone who only walks between their car and their desk that once broken in bench-made shoes are extremely comfortable."

PANTHERELLA

"Men are willing to wear brighter, more interesting 'statement' socks now than they used to, and even formal socks have become more casual. Though thankfully we're still not talking novelty here—no SpongeBob SquarePants please," advises Justin Hall, fifth-generation managing director of the British sock manufacturer H.J. Socks—founded in Leicester, UK, in 1937 by Louis Goldschmidt, pioneer of the lightweight sock—and owner of the Pantherella brand. Pantherella socks are made on both Victorian and ultra-modern machines that knit with between a 96 and 240 needle construction—the more needles required, the finer the sock but the slower it is to make and so the more expensive it is—and in differing yarns, including luxury Sea Island Cotton and, a first in the sock business, Escorial. Each production run also goes through a quality control lab where it is tested for abrasion, tension, and consistency of color. Small wonder H.J. has also made socks for the likes of Richard James, Barney's New York, and Brooks Brothers.

CHEANEY

The Oxford is one of the oldest styles of dress shoe—the archetype of the business shoe. And Joseph Cheaney & Sons, established near Northampton, England in 1886, is one of the style's oldest makers—using cork cushioning for comfort and the traditional Goodyear welting that allows a sole to be both waterproof and repeatedly replaced when it wears out. The company, once owned by Prada along with sister brand Church's, is now run and owned by Jonathan and William Church, of the Church's family. But conservative styles are not its only forte: Cheaney is likely to produce what William Church calls "shoes with a twist, for the guy who likes the quality of English-made shoes but is also much more conscious now of the way his shoes look, and who wants something more modern."

FESTIVE

FESTIVE
CLOTHING

HERE'S TO YOU

THERE IS ALWAYS A REASON TO CELEBRATE—EVEN IF IT'S JUST LIFE ITSELF. TODAY, AS MEN'S TIES ARE LOOSENED AND STRICT DRESS CODES NO LONGER ENFORCED, MEN HAVE BECOME MORE DARING AND WILLING TO EXPERIMENT THAN EVER.

by
NATHANIEL ADAMS

Festivities, occasions, parties, bashes, dos, call them what you will, present the perfect opportunity for a man to dress up. Dressing well is partly a matter of dressing for the occasion, and the way a man dresses for a celebration should naturally be celebratory. Fortunately, the past several years have seen a rediscovery and re-appreciation of older, time-honored brands as well as a veritable explosion of new clothing labels and designers with fresh takes on traditional themes and a feel for flair

The man of the third millennium has emerged from a brief dark age of shlubishness into the nova-bright glare of a men's fashion renaissance.

and innovation that keeps pace with the multi-trend global sartoriosphere, traveling as it does at the speed of Instagram. The best of these companies combines a deep knowledge of history, technique, craft, and tradition with an understanding of the artistry and excitement of runway fashion. The man of the third millennium has emerged from a brief dark age of shlubishness into the nova-bright glare of a men's fashion renaissance and

so far, things are looking good for his style. He may have to wear a suit to work on Wall Street or a t-shirt and shorts to work in Silicon Valley or leather chaps and a harness to work in the red-light district, but festivities are when his inner dandy can shine through, whether through a bespoke suit, a flashy pair of socks, or a rakish hat.

There was a time when what we now call "dressing up," was simply called "dressing." Photographs and paintings show us that the past had a strict dress code, and one can imagine a time traveler from a previous century—or even decade—asking what sort of crisis—environmental, financial, or moral—led to today's fashion pastiche, eclecticism, semi-nudity, and exaltation of comfort.

The old sartorial formalism is the idea of "occasion" taken to its purest and most austere conclusion: rules and regulations abound—an arcane horoscope tracking season, hour, location, status, function, and company, and prescribing colors, styles, materials, and cut. But, as our collars have softened down through the decades so have the lines between these occasions. Some might lament the loss of a mythical golden past of smart and neat men in neckties, but what we've sacrificed in buttoned-up formality we've gained in sartorial freedom. We live in a time of unprecedented choice in clothing, fashion, and style, and as a result people put more thought into their outfits than ever before—even if that outfit consists of sneakers, jeans, and a t-shirt.

All this is to say that a world without dress codes, unburdened by mandatory formality, is a good thing. Some men have used the dissolution of the rules to stop thinking about their clothes entirely, letting themselves go like an unbelted gut after a big meal. But more and more are exploring elegance in personal dress, and if the first reaction to freedom is the ecstatic spurning of the rules, a closer examination and appreciation of the thought behind those rules can yield new understanding and fertile ground for innovation. Now that men don't have to dress up, they get to dress up.

The look itself is young and celebratory, and it appreciates tradition without being ruled by it. Sharply-tailored suits and jackets, playful colors and patterns, well-polished shoes with a rich patina in ombre shades, lapel pins and jewelry both cheeky and elegant, neckwear as eclectic in style and inspiration as it is varied in material and construction—these are some of the elements of this new global style.

Festivities needn't be formal, but their aim is celebration, even simply (and most importantly) of life in general rather than a specific occasion, and aside from the brands new and old, there's a sup-

Some might lament the loss of a mythical golden past of smart and neat men in neckties, but what we've sacrificed in buttoned-up formality we've gained in sartorial freedom.

port structure of books *(I am Dandy: The Return of the Elegant Gentleman, Bespoke: The Men's Style of Savile Row)*, blogs *(Gentleman's Gazette, Articles of Style)*, magazines *(The Rake, Jocks and Nerds)*, and social media accounts with the sole aim of sharing and celebrating the new sartorialism.

The availability of the elements of this style has increased across the board and at many price points. At the higher end of things, multi-brand shops like The Armoury in Hong Kong and New York create a shopping experience that combines the best of boutique and department store shopping. The Armoury's staff is an international team of young menswear experts and enthusiasts who live the very lifestyle they promote. The product buys are diverse and far ranging enough to be interesting while nevertheless creating a very cohesive "look" from various brands that becomes, in turn, The Armoury's own brand. From shoes to scarves to perfume to pants, the brands championed and stocked by The Armoury are always perfectly aesthetically complementary. And The Armoury takes their commitment as something of an intermediary company very seriously—organizing dozens of trunk shows in several locations each year, bringing artisans, designers, and craftspeople directly to the customer, fostering a type of shopping based on personal relationships.

Shops like Zurich's AP&Co and London's Present have a similar approach with a rather less formal result. These shops understand that to be truly successful today and inspire loyalty to one's brand one has to sell a lifestyle along with the clothing. It's why stores like this sometimes carry books, stationery, pocketknives, magazines, special liquor, and even—

Now that men don't have to dress up they get to dress up.

in the case of AP&Co—a handmade mushroom scavenging calendar. The creators of these shops have invented an ideal customer and stocked up on everything he needs, and the people who shop there have responded well.

Some boutiques have a narrower focus but are no less expert or dedicated to both product and customer. Leffot in New York is the perfect example of a store devoted to shoes of the best quality and design, expertly sourced and sold by Steven Taffel. From big names in traditional shoemaking like Alden and Church's to lesser-known shoemakers like J. Fitzpatrick and Enzo Bonafe, Taffel makes sure that Leffot carries beautiful shoes which can't be found anywhere else in the city—all in one place.

For those on a more modest budget there are places like The Fine and Dandy Shop—both a brick–and-mortar store in New York City and an online shop—which specializes in a wide range of their own brand of men's accessories as well as books, cosmetics, and various other odds and ends, and a continually updating, expertly sourced collection of vintage and antique items for sale.

The ease of internet shopping has, of course, had an effect on menswear and the ability of new designers and producers to market their own products directly to the customer and press. Larger websites like Mr. Porter and Gilt Man offer designer menswear at a fraction of the price. And small, niche brands like some of those in this chapter have found the internet to be the perfect place to launch their brands and acquire a loyal clientele.

The time and conditions are perfect for a new male sartorial flourishing and that's exactly what we're seeing. Whether it will be a lasting phenomenon or simply one brief trend among many remains to be seen, but the sheer scale and volume of the move toward a dandy-positive fashion aesthetic is encouraging.

For years, well-dressed men have been asked, "What's the special occasion?" The cleverer among us are realizing that "life" is the best answer.

PAUL STUART

Founded in 1938, Paul Stuart is proud of its heritage, and not without reason. Although it started somewhat later than the other iconic American brands that came to define the "Ivy League" look of the early 20th Century, such as Brooks Brothers, Oxxford, J. Press, and Hickey Freeman, Paul Stuart can and still does lay claim to being a part of that remarkably influential sea change in menswear. But where Paul Stuart differs from the others is that at some point around the 1970s it began to shift slightly away from the comfortable familiarity of what had become the look of the American establishment and toward a more cosmopolitan feel, becoming less like a traditional haberdasher and more like a fashion label. The rebranding, reinventing, and marketing of the Ivy League look with an eye to the fashion market was smart— Ralph Lauren has built a multi-label fashion empire in his Anglo-Americana style, and in recent years the original Ivy League brands have attempted to do the same by hiring hot new designers to produce diffusion lines targeting a younger, more runway-savvy clientele. But Paul Stuart has done it with a natural ease.

The main line of Paul Stuart tailored suiting is traditional in its foundations of various grays, blues, and browns.

But it stands out by virtue of details which go beyond the typical dress code of the boardroom or the White House— a few peaked lapels, English-inspired ticket pockets, and the occasional plaid or windowpane pattern. The sport coats are often made of blended fabrics—silks, wools, linens, tweeds—sometimes in particularly interesting weaves, more exciting than the usual brass-buttoned navy blazer or madras plaid jacket one might find at Brooks Brothers.

But what really stands out at Paul Stuart is Phineas Cole. Started in 2007, Phineas Cole was the first and only extension line Paul Stuart has ever produced, and it couldn't have come at a better time. Recognizing the explosion in interest in tailored menswear from young men, the line caters to a consumer who appreciates the quality and know-how that comes with heritage and tradition but seeks a more daring and dandyish aesthetic. A Phineas Cole jacket is a slimmer cut with a more pronounced waist, high armholes, and a soft shoulder. Common details are peaked lapels with a very high gorge and sharply slanted hacking pockets, adding to the X-shaped angularity of the silhouette, designed to make a man look broad-shouldered but slim without padding or Spanx-like modern corsetry.

But the beauty of Phineas Cole, as expressed under the direction of designer Ralph Auriemma, not only comes out in the shape but in the substance: exquisite fabrics, light but never flimsy in summer, strong but never stiff in autumn, and often featuring rich colors—jewel-toned purples, crimsons, and greens—echoed in the neckties. Paul Stuart's neckties and pocket squares—Phineas Cole's in

New at Paul Stuart

particular—are gems often overlooked when the brand is discussed. Auriemma's expert eye for art deco patterns—interlocking diamonds, dazzling print-like triangle repeats, Japanese-esque fans, staggering zigzags—make each season's ties stand out from the classic fare found at Paul Stuart's Madison Avenue neighbors. The Phineas Cole ties are—aside from being very reasonably priced— well made, and they're styled in the look books with a small four-in-hand knot that emphasizes the bloom of the tie's blade, which proudly springs forward off the chest, a detail that looks particularly good with the slashing cutaway collars of Phineas Cole shirts. The whole effect is one of an immediately recognizable signature style, a somewhat devilish riff on typical Madison Avenue preppy— a colorful rake painted in dandy angles. The Victoriana coup de grace sometimes added to the Phineas Cole look is the double-breasted odd vest with shawl lapel and keystone button placement, a rarely seen item in other stores.

The Paul Stuart flagship store on Madison Avenue is an impressive multistory emporium with Phineas Cole occupying the top floor. They also have several Japanese locations, two shops in Chicago, and, most recently, a shop in Washington D.C., with plans to open more locations in U.S. cities in the coming years. Paul Stuart has never been as widely known as Brooks Brothers or Ralph Lauren, and young runway-watchers will usually say "do you mean Paul Smith?" But with plans for expansion and Phineas Cole leading the charge toward a more adventurous aesthetic the brand may be entering a new era and more men's wardrobes.

GIEVES & HAWKES

Savile Row, after two stubborn centuries spent acquiring a reputation for stodgy conservatism and old-fashioned fuddy-duddery, has had a remarkable resurgence in recent years. In the past decade or so the Row, and many of the venerable houses on it, have come together to market themselves as the collective home of British tailoring, proudly proclaiming their heritage and establishment connections while remodeling their businesses to compete in the world of fashion. Perhaps no Savile Row house has done this as well as Gieves & Hawkes, which has made a new reputation for itself as a smart and respective ready-to-wear label while still remaining true to its roots and credentials as a bespoke tailor of the highest quality—a challenging balance to strike.

Thomas Hawkes set up his first London shop in 1771, establishing himself as a tailor and gaining a large military clientele. James Watson Gieve began his career as a naval tailor in Portsmouth in 1835. Hawkes & Co. moved to their present location at No. 1, Savile Row in 1912 and they only combined with Gieves & Co. in 1974. Between them the companies have an impressive historical roster of clients, picking up several Royal Warrants for their work as military outfitters along the way. Gieves made the coat that Admiral Nelson died in and Gieves & Hawkes made the iconic and dazzling frogged and embroidered frock coat Michael Jackson wore in the 1980s.

In recent years Gieves & Hawkes has repositioned itself, trading on its reputation for fine tailoring to market itself as a lifestyle brand for a refined modern gentleman with a taste for elegance. The ready-to-wear clothing remains dignified and reasonably restrained, never approaching flamboyance, but without the repeated aspirational appeal to an ideal of "luxury" so commonly relied on by mainstream runway fashion labels. Gieves & Hawkes' quintessential Britishness is in its calm but proper style.

Gieves & Hawkes ready-to-wear is reasonably priced at rather less than half what a bespoke suit tends to cost on Savile Row. What the company has done so well in its approach to selling ready-to-wear is to always keep the company's bespoke credentials in the customer's mind. It's true that they sell suits online, but the brand always suggests that customers come to their stores in person—make an appointment, even—and their level of customer service and attention goes some way to recreating the experience of a bespoke suit fitting, at least in terms of personal attention. A man who can't afford either the time, money, or both needed to have a bespoke suit made can still expect a similar level of care and seriousness when he goes to Gieves & Hawkes for an off-the-peg suit.

In these days of "vertical integration" and the one-stop shop, brands are under pressure to diversify, to do everything, lest the customer spend any of his wardrobe budget elsewhere. Gieves & Hawkes has gone down this path, making t-shirts, polo shirts, ties, knitwear, belts, shoes, socks, denim, and cufflinks. It's the curse of the aspiring lifestyle brand to seek completeness, producing enough kinds of things to fill a look book or at least dress a model head to toe. Gieves & Hawkes expanding range of non-tailored clothing and accessories is well made from beautiful materials, but the same confident restraint they bring to their suits can look a bit flat and uninspired in a t-shirt, especially at that price. There's no real reason a suit company should necessarily make terrific socks or turtleneck sweaters, and if Gieves & Hawkes casual wear is something of a sideshow that's ok, because they make excellent suits. What they do better than others is reason enough to seek them out.

An example of what Gieves & Hawkes really does best is formal wear. Everybody maxes tuxedoes (although not usually as well,) but there are very few places to buy morning suits and jackets off the peg at this high a quality. It's true that many men don't usually get summonses to traditional English daytime weddings, much less the Royal Ascot races, but the fact that Gieves & Hawkes makes such an offering should be an indication of how seriously they take the more buttoned-up brand of festivity.

GAZIANO & GIRLING

Tradition goes a long way in menswear marketing—customers who pay top dollar for items often like to know that they have a heritage, a pedigree, some continuity with time-honored methods. Nowhere is this more true than in

England, where a brand's reputation can be founded almost entirely on a lengthy history. The shoemakers Gaziano & Girling do not have a centuries-old history. Founded in 2006 by Tony Gaziano and Dean Girling, they've barely been around a decade. But in that relatively

short time, they've shown that a respect for traditional methods combined with a flair for innovation in design can trump a long timeline studded with Royal Warrants in the here and now.

Gaziano and Girling have many years experience between them working with the finest shoemakers in England— G.J. Cleverley, John Lobb, and Edward Green. These venerable firms have long histories and set the standard in terms of quality. But their reputations are largely thanks to their fine bespoke work, and their ready-to-wear collections often stay on the safe side of dandyism. One of Gaziano & Girling's main aims is to not only bring the high quality of bespoke footwear to ready-to-wear but also to offer something close to the range of style and fit found in the bespoke process.

The company began by focusing on bespoke shoes with a large client base in Japan, but after great initial success and increased demand, Gaziano and Girling began making ready-to-wear shoes, eventually opening their own factory in 2013 and a flagship store on Savile Row. Gaziano & Girling shoes are now sold in fine boutiques and department stores around the world, as well as on their website (although the online store has a limited selection that tends toward the traditional style).

What makes Gaziano & Girling so excellent is their combination of English craftsmanship with Italian style.

Their shoes are comfortable, and each last is available in five widths and half-sizes, offering a rare range of fit. The uppers are most often made from French

and Swiss calf leather, chosen from the best sections of hide and finished in Italy. Their soles are made of traditional oak-bark leather made in ancient Roman tanning pits in Devon, and they're Goodyear welted using Barbour threads with a high number of stitches.

All of this fancy-sounding production partly appeals to the luxury and craft-fetishist crowds, but it does genuinely mean that their shoes are very well made and it goes some way to justifying the high price tag (a basic pair of ready-to-wear shoes goes for around 900 GBP). But, quality aside, what sets them apart

from and above so many other luxury shoe companies is the boldness of their designs. Their lasts are slim and elegant, with a tight Italian waist and a softened angular shape. Their leathers are richly colored, and they particularly excel at imparting beautiful patinas, so much so that two members of their shop staff are "master patineurs," according to Tony Gaziano, who offer customers their choice of beautifully blended colors, including nine suggested combinations demonstrated on an assortment of slip-ons in the store.

Generally speaking, there are lots of classic styles in their main collection—Oxfords, derbys, single and double monks, penny and tassel loafers, Balmoral and Chelsea boots, and casual slip-ons with elasticized sides—but they stand out in their details: here a grained calf leather, there an unusually curved seam, perhaps a flourishing brogueing on a toe, a deep and smooth patina, or a contrasting suede. These are all available from stock or made to order in any of their several lasts.

Standing out from this is their Deco collection, introduced in 2011, which features a "spade waist" that comes in very tight from the heel before sweeping out into the elongated front of the shoe. The Deco shoes are breathtakingly elegant in their shape—shark-like and thrilling, they're slick demons in shoe form, devilish and decadent, and arguably one of the most beautiful ranges of shoes available today. Gaziano & Girling also have a range of formal shoes that includes slippers and pumps in velvet or patent leather and the Cornwell, a stand-out formal shoe of streamlined and seamless black patent leather laced up with a red silk ribbon like a gift.

Gaziano & Girling shoes are generally outside the shoe budget of the average man, but that's because they're above-average shoes. Price tag aside they should still be recognized and praised, because if a company like this can grow and succeed, they may go on to someday set the standard for traditional quality and innovative design for shoemakers across the board, which would be a good thing for the future of our feet.

CHARVET

In the menswear lexicon the words luxury, heritage, elegance, and craftsmanship have been left pale from repeated bloodlettings by unoriginal copywriters. How fortunate then, that in one case all these and more can be said with a single, unembellished word: Charvet. Charvet has, for more than 150 years, been the ne plus ultra of excellence in men's attire and furnishings, one of the last remaining links to the material and aesthetic world of France's greatest flowering of dandyism, and the bearer of an unmatched historical—and, more uniquely, cultural—pedigree.

Founded in Paris in 1838 as a shirt-maker, Charvet focused on quality, style, and innovation, not only by using new methods in construction and design, but by creating a one-stop emporium, simplifying things for the customer while ensuring careful oversight of the entire shirt-making process under one roof. By the time Charvet moved to the first of its iconic homes on the Place Vendome in 1877, the company already had a reputation as the best in the world. Its client list read like a Who's Who of the international aristocracy, and orders were being taken from as far afield as New Orleans and St. Petersburg.

With the same attention to detail and design the firm devoted to continuously developing new silk, cotton, and linen shirtings, Charvet began producing handkerchiefs, pajamas, dressing gowns, scarves, silk knot cufflinks (which they invented), waistcoats (possibly being the first to popularize them with shawl lapels), and, most famously, neckties, which are draped and hung all over the Place Vendome store's ground floor like rainbow waterfalls.

artist in creation," Charvet ties appear in the works of Marcel Proust, Dorothy Parker, Somerset Maugham, Ian Fleming, P.G. Wodehouse, Evelyn Waugh, Anthony Burgess, William Gibson, and Tom Wolfe. Sometimes they are symbols of beauty and a character's refinement, at other times they are less flattering symbols of unabashed materialism or shallowness—a Charvet tie can be shorthand for elegance or its bastard half-brother extravagance.

The frisson of purchasing, unwrapping, and knotting a Charvet tie is more than purely aesthetic or tactile, it can make the owner and wearer feel like part of an intellectual, even psychological legacy. Those who've fallen under the Charvet spell include French statesmen from DeGaulle to Mitterrand to Sarkozy to Chirac, English leaders from Edward VII and VIII through Churchill and Prince Charles, and the more stylish American presidents, including Truman, Kennedy, Reagan, and Obama. Poets from Baudelaire to Betjeman and novelists from Zola to Hemingway have worn Charvet, as have artists such as Matisse, Monet, and Manet, and actors including Fred Astaire, Gary Cooper, Orson Welles, Yul Brenner, Jeremy Irons, Adolphe Manjou, and Bruce Willis. Notable female Charvet devotees include George Sand, Gertrude Stein, Coco Chanel, Fran Lebowitz, Daphne Guinness, Uma Thurman, Faye Dunaway, and Jane Birkin. Musicians as diverse as Berlioz, Debussy, Offenbach, and Brian Ferry have shopped at Place Vendome. Occultist Aleister Crowley was a customer, as were the architects Frank Lloyd Wright and Sanford White. Some of today's notable Charvet wearers are Vogue editor Hamish Bowles, New York Police Commissioner Raymond Kelly, white-collar swindler Bernie Madoff, and French philosophe Bernard Henri-Levy, who famously has his shirts specially made with a secret gravity-defying construction method so the collars will remain standing even when the shirt front has been unbuttoned.

To be sure, a trip to the shop today wouldn't be complete without seeing the famous mur des blancs on the third floor, where bolts of thousands of shirting fabrics are available in hundreds of shades of white for the production of bespoke shirts (and an examination of the skill with which stripes are lined up on their shirts should leave no doubt as to their quality). But in the 20th century, Charvet's woven silk neckties, produced in countless patterns, colors, shapes, and weaves, were shipped to shops and worn by clients around the world, spreading the name and knowledge of Charvet and making it the byword for beauty that it is today.

There is something special about a Charvet necktie. It is sumptuous and elegant, perhaps not an everyday item for every man, but something undeniably refined and precious. It is a rare thing to find such a perfect single item in a man's wardrobe possessed of all the sculptural and tactile qualities of fine jewelry. But the beautifully woven silk of a Charvet necktie (including, but not limited to, the company's signature "Charvet" weave, a variation on the classic regence weave) can simultaneously flow like water and, owing to its fine construction, stand as firm as crystal. Charvet's current director, Jean-Claude Colban, says that what makes a Charvet tie so distinct and excellent is the weave of the silk and the way it plays with the light: "a beautiful necktie is like a jewel."

As you can see, it can be difficult to resist the urge to rhapsodize and open oneself to charges of hyperbole. But I wouldn't be the first to fall under the charm of Charvet. Jean Cocteau said that Charvet is "where the rainbow finds ideas," James McNeil Whistler called Charvet "the greatest

When someone buys and wears a piece of Charvet, they can still feel a part of this sartorial continuum without having to actually own a rare and costly historical or antique item. Charvet has, in its name and its make, more than a "heritage" that most other brands would dream of: it has a romance all its own.

DOYLE MUESER

Doyle Mueser is at the leading edge of a wave of new and sophisticated bespoke suit makers run by young people around the world but specifically in New York City. Owners Amber Doyle and Jake Mueser combine an eye for trends in men's fashion with a commitment to employing the finest tailors and cutters for their bespoke creations. Their seasonal ready-to-wear collections show an easily adapted house style that embraces elements of English, American, and Italian tailoring traditions, but when it comes to bespoke their flexibility and knack for creating precisely what their client wants and needs is impressive. This talent for personal, unique creations, as well as their own connections to New York's art, fashion, music, and media scenes has made them an increasingly popular choice for custom suits for actors, musicians, artists, and other members of New York's young creative class.

JEFFREY-WEST

Jeffery-West shoes are gleefully and proudly not for everyone. Although made in Northampton. England, home of traditional British cordwaining, with the same attention to craftsmanship and quality as many of the more mainstream shoemakers in the area, Jeffery West's designs are outlandish, provocative, and very rock 'n' roll. The lasts are long, usually on the pointier side, often with a chisel toe. The brogueing is done with diamond-shaped punches in patterns like the Maltese Cross. Styles are available in unusual leathers in high-shine finishes, faux reptile skins, bright and swirled colors, metallic, skull prints, embossed paisleys and lightning bolts. But among the high-zip boots with Cuban heels (cloven hooves, actually) and Ziggy Stardust in-spired showpieces are well-made oxfords, loafers, Chelsea boots, and monk-straps with just enough rock 'n' roll shape and style to suit the dapper man who wants to show how his wild side walks with him.

DENTS

Dents, established in 1777, is a leather goods brand whose heritage is as unimpeachable as its quality. They make wallets, purses, belts, and more, but they're best known for their gloves, which are unrivaled in variety, style, and craftsmanship, well suited to many different functions and occasions. Their gloves are made from hairsheep leather, deerskin, suede, peccary, lambskin, and nubuck, and lined with fleece, silk, cashmere, chamois, and fur. The various models are also usually available in several shades of brown and gray as well as occasional options in red, yellow, tan, aubergine, green, navy, and more. Details and options abound: knitted cuffs, buttoning straps, crochet backs for driving gloves, fingerless models, Harris tweed panels, sidewalls and piping in contrasting leathers, zippers, hunting and shooting mitts, quilting, and models constructed for use with touchscreens. The sheer variety of their offerings is staggering, and a man would be hard-pressed not to find the right glove for his needs, be they dress, sport, driving, or casual.

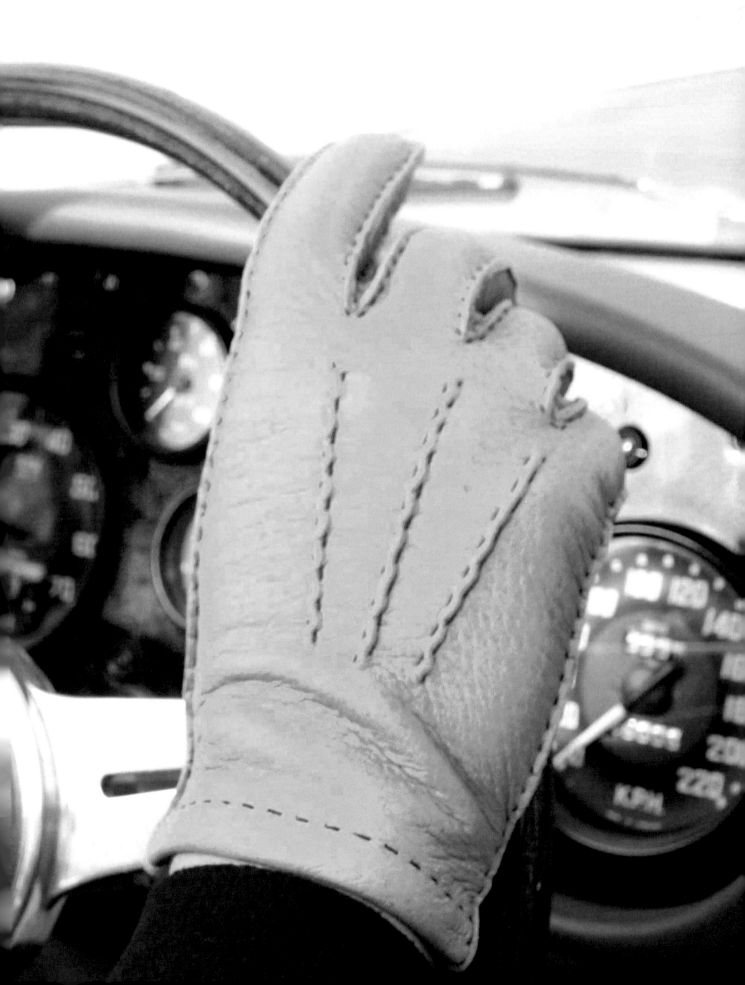

D.S. &
DURGA

In an office in a converted warehouse building in the Gowanus neighborhood of Brooklyn (named after the filthy river that flows through it), D.S. & Durga creates fragrances that evoke worlds beyond the toxic miasma outside. D.S. & Durga perfumes and colognes are rich and deep, and their Proustian ability to conjure mood and memory is as much a result of their process of creation as of the ingredients themselves. At the workshop, the component scents are organized in an antique card file with drawers labeled not with the contents or even their category, but with impressions—a drawer marked with a specific 19th century date, another with a place, another with a reference to music or poetry. D.S. & Durga has a wide range of fragrances and continues to develop new scents (including the Hylands range, inspired by a pseudo-historical and mythopoetic look at the British Isles) and collaborations (most recently the Longshoreman cologne exclusive with J. Crew).

BY
ELIAS

By Elias jewelry is the creation of Bevin Elias, a supremely stylish and oft-photographed New Yorker with a long history working in menswear. By Elias makes lovely cufflinks and tie bars, but their star items are their lapel pins—glittering gold and silver accents for any occasion that calls for an extra flash of character. Their subjects reminiscent of spring—large and small blooming roses in gold and silver, regal fleur de lis, and flying bees ready to pollinate. By Elias is all about the details, partly because a lapel pin is a detail itself—the punctuation to the statement one's outfit is making. Even in the design, the details are seen in the variety. There isn't just one bee pin, there are Ethiopian honeybees, a slightly more rustic antiquarian "Abielle Bee," and the "Rebellious Bee." All are available in gold or silver, and the Rebellious Bee is available with black enamel stripes or in a more luxurious version studded with cubic zirconias.

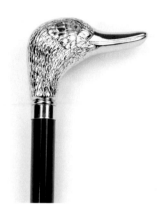

FOX
UMBRELLAS

All too often the umbrella is overlooked as an important accessory for a man of style. It's true that the once-ubiquitous walking stick is now a rather pimpish affectation for a man without a limp, but an umbrella fills a similar aesthetic function while retaining a universal utility (at least in places where it rains once in a while). Fox Umbrellas was founded in 1868, and it remains the gold standard among umbrella makers, not only because it makes them well (the company has a range of different makes at a broad selection of price points) but also because it has a level of customization typically found at bespoke clothing shops. A gentleman can choose between automatic and manual frames, classic slim tube frames or solid single-wood handles in varying woods and stains and shapes—oak, rosewood, maple, malacca, chestnut, hazel, ash, etc—as well as special handles—nickel, gold, and silver-plated details, leather wrapped, inlaid with horn, or shaped like animal heads. The covers themselves are available in many colors and prints, and the ambitious umbrella purchaser can avail himself of their bespoke service and design his own, down to the color of his canopy's hem.

SECRET EMPIRE

Dr. Lee-Jon Ball and Nathaniel Adams started Secret Empire with the aim of creating a personal bespoke experience of good quality aimed at like-minded men and at a price point that won't intimidate the novice suit wearer while still reminding them that suiting is serious work. Secret Empire is based on a desire to make suits for people they like—people like them, and every client becomes a member of the Empire, a participant in a cheeky sartorial ritual. When they come out the other side they're better dressed, better informed, and, more often than not, considerably drunker than when they went in (on both whiskey and power, but never on Powers Whiskey). Secret Empire suits are modern but with the occasional respectful bow to past styles, as in their signature Victorianesque double-breasted shawl lapel waistcoat with keystone button placement. Secret Empire seeks to revive this sadly neglected style that so perfectly makes the trim-waist-ed and broad-shouldered silhouette of the roguish hero.

POST IMPERIAL

Post Imperial is an accessories brand founded by New York-based Nigerian designer Niyi Okuboyejo. Post Imperial produces a seasonal range of scarves, ties, and pocket squares in silk, cotton, linen, wool, and cashmere, most of them made using a traditional hand-dyeing process practiced by the Yoruba women of South-western Nigeria called adire. Unlike other resist-dyeing processes like batik, which uses wax, adire uses a paste made of starch from the Cassava root. The combination of Okuboyejo's modern designs and this ancient and almost vanished technique results in beautiful ghost-edged patterns with rich natural colors. The pieces feature abstract shapes: galactic whorls, spattered dots, squiggly waves, and splintered lines, thick block stripes, zigzags, diamonds, and coronal spots, as well as the odd figurative flower or bird. Many of the superbly made pieces have unfinished fringed edges, well suited to the brand's fusion of elegance and handicraft.

CARUSO

Caruso is a relatively new brand, sprung from branches of the Brioni tree, which went in its own direction. The brand shows a playfulness, rare in far too many menswear brands. Their mannequins have cartoonish faces, each character given a name and personal style. They use long silk neck scarves instead of ties some times. They make silk-fringed wallets to be worn in the breast pocket of a suit jacket, peeking out like a pocket square.

And they work in beautiful colors and materials, for example, a tomato soup-colored duffel coat with a chinchilla collar. One standout piece from a recent collection is a white dinner jacket made entirely of silk grosgrain, the ribbing running horizontally. The item exemplifies the design philosophy of Caruso—elegant, classic, and of the highest quality, but going slightly against the grain—in this case quite literally.

DRAKE'S

Drake's is, simply put, one of the greatest tie companies in the world. They make other clothes, too, but their ties, made in England by people who have spent their whole lives making ties, are exceptional. Drake's ties tend toward the understated—not big, shiny, thickly woven silks with power knots, but soft and deep colors, often in fabric blends incorporating wool, cotton, dupioni, shantung, or cashmere, always well balanced with an interlining that perfectly complements the weight and thickness of the tie's fabric.

Drake's makes ties for tie lovers—necktie nerds, perhaps. Their printed Ancient Madder silk ties have an unmatched depth and richness of color, albeit muted with a slight dustiness imparted to them by the vegetable dyes used. Whereas their ties tend toward abstract and classic patterns, their scarves and pocket squares are often canvases for figurative scenes, icons, and characters: dance step diagrams, flamingos with sunglasses and beach furniture, corgi dogs, skiers, or warring Central Asian hordes.

CORGI

Although usually one of the first things a man puts on, socks are often the last thing a man thinks of when shopping for new clothes. Indeed, the acquisition of hosiery is sometimes foregone, forsworn, and left to the dependable generosity of maiden aunts and the like. But when it comes to festivities, dressing up, and adding character to an outfit, the sock is an item that punches above its weight in wool. Corgi is a Welsh company founded in 1892 that makes excellent socks and has recently come to greater attention in the U.S. thanks to a collaboration with J. Crew. Corgi socks come in hundreds of seasonal styles, each usually in several colorways: thick hand-cabled cashmere socks, Fair Isle patterns, fine-gauge cashmere and silk dress hose, and socks in wool, cottons, and blends featuring stripes, spots, diamonds, zigzags, monograms, and animals in vivid colors. Even the most conservative dresser can make his feet fit for an occasion by showing a flash of style at his ankles.

NACKYMADE

Despite the fact that more than half of the population of most Western countries wears some kind of corrective lenses, eyeglasses get short shrift in style guides. But spectacles are big business in the fashion world, and you'd be hard-pressed to find a serious fashion label that didn't also do some kind of eyewear. But some of the freshest, most fun, original, and exciting glasses in the world are made by Naoki Nakagawa, a.k.a. "Nacky," a self-taught eyeglass maker who makes ready-to-wear, made-to-order, and bespoke frames. Nacky's frames are available in classic styles in a variety of materials including woods, metals, and acetates in various marbled and colored configurations. The customization goes beyond the color, size, and shape of the frames to the colors and material of the hinges, the nose pads, and– the most stylish part of Nacky's glasses—the stems, which are available in many elegant and sometimes playful shapes, including triceratops, dragons, tailoring shears, and fish, among other things.

HVRMINN & CO

HVRMINN is a relatively new and small brand from New York City. It offers individual be-spoke appointments in its studio in Manhattan's garment district, but its seasonal ready-to-wear collections show the serious design chops of a brand to watch. HVRMINN's tailored mens-wear line, EPONYMOVS, features serious-looking suits, sharply cut with strong angles, usually in bold masculine colors—slate grays, bloody burgundies, earthy camelhairs, and dis-tinguished navies. The brand's cuts are usually very slim, and it can sometimes seem a bit too devoted to the Thom Brownesque, short, Pee Wee pants style, but one of the most striking things about its garments is how well balanced they are, with neatly struck angles to their la-pels, hems, and pockets, particularly on the double-breasted suits, which are executed with perfect proportions between the button stance and the jacket waist, especially on the difficult-to-pull–off, low, single-button jackets. Its mil-itary-inspired outerwear line, Vietto, pays the same exceptional level of attention to parkas, duffel coats, and the like.

LAIRD HATTERS

The hat has made a comeback in recent years, despite a minor online backlash depicting fedora-wearers as hopelessly uncool nerds playing at sophistication. A brimmed hat may not be the simplest starting point for an aspiring dandy, but it is something he can learn to incorporate (an easy system involves wearing no more than two of the following three facial accessories at a time: facial hair, glasses, hat). Some of the great old hat companies, including Borsalino and Stetson, have introduced updated and less conservative models recently. But among new hat brands, Laird of London is doing an exemplary job of balancing the classic with the daring. Laird offers a wide range, from tweed country hats with leather detailing to formal top hats to various flat caps and Panamas, but their best items are their fur felt fedoras and trilbies, blocked in rakish shapes, available in beautiful colors and a range of variation in detail that covers not only the width of the brim and its snap but the width of the grosgrain band and its color, too. You can't go wrong with their signature trilby, a fur felt hat in a suede finish with a slim grosgrain band and a smoothly angled brim, available in rich colors including pink, green, and burgundy.

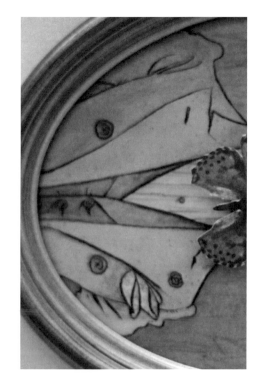

LE LOIR EN PAPILLON

Mickael Loir makes beautiful silk scarves and bow ties (the brand's name comes from his enthusiasm for that accessory as well as his passion for lepidoptery). But Loir's most beautiful and unique creations are his lapel pins—a whimsical and fantastic assortment of pieces made with precious and semi-precious materials: flowers in mother of pearl, felt, quartz, lapis lazuli, and Swarovski crystal, grinning skulls in antler, amethyst, rock crystal, and bone (each with a metal mesh bow tie under its jaw) , colorful enamel on metal flying insects, beetles preserved under glass, small glass vases to be worn behind the lapel so a boutonnière can stay fresh in water for longer, and a long-lashed, blinking doll's eyeball. Rounding out Loir's gorgeous offerings are limited edition series of pocket squares—a series of imperial caricatures, including Louis XVI and Marie Antoinette by the artist Alban Guillemois; a series of entomological illustrations by artist Eve Raspberry; and a pastel portrait of a Parisian dandy by Massimiliano Mocchia di Coggiola.

GAME, SET, AND MATCH

FOR MANY YEARS, SPORTSWEAR WAS MADE TO BE UNIFORM AND FUNCTIONAL. WITH GROWING INTEREST IN HEALTH AND FITNESS, SPORTSWEAR MADE ITS WAY INTO OUR EVERYDAY LIVES AND NOW MANIFESTS ITSELF AS HIGH FASHION.

by

OMAR MUÑOZ CREMERS

In ancient Greece, physical exercise was considered an integral part of life. Many sports of that era were rediscovered in the 19th century. Together with the introduction of a number of new sports, this would eventually lead to the modern rebirth of the Olympic Games. One important difference stands out between the ages: Hellenic men practiced most sports naked. Modern sport thus heralded the birth of sportswear, almost at the same time as Victorian mores imposed swimwear on naked swimmers. Although sport gained popularity thanks to the introduction of leisure time, it has often been remarked that the activity also forms a mostly harmless substitution for war. This military aspect continued in clothing. In team sports, the uniform was introduced to distinguish the opponent as one would an enemy army, while other sports, like hockey, developed protective garments with the same function as armor.

Everyday fashion and sportswear remained separated domains until well into the 1970s. Early companies like Champion, Le Coq Sportif, and Adidas manufactured functional garments and shoes, often for specific sports. Some preliminary crossover occurred when the Lacoste polo shirt became a casual alternative for the shirt in the preppy style of the Ivy League universities. Made of high quality piqué the Lacoste polo could be easily worn under a sweater or jacket, giving men new options for dressing in a stylish but less formal manner. The growing professionalism and media interest in sports, combined with the practice of sport as a hobby, resulted in an explosive growth in sport apparel. A crucial crossover gained momentum in the mid-1970s when the sneaker started to be worn as everyday footwear, turning some brands into multinationals whose reputation rivaled the world's biggest companies. Sponsorship deals with popular players like Michael Jordan would elevate them into style icons rivaling pop stars or actors. A new American style was created by combining hoodies, satin Starter jackets, and baseball caps. The classic Champion hoodie, which until the 1990s was hard to find in Europe, would eventually rival the conventional sweater. Earlier, the Converse All-Stars had become all the rage. All-Stars, or the lower Superga 2750 alternative from Italy, were often combined with Levi's jeans and a down vest. The spread of the down vest and jacket was a direct result of the growing popularity of winter sports. The down jacket to this day retains its popularity although the silhouette is not as extreme as it used to be (Moncler Gamme Bleu's mix of haute couture and sportswear today remains a singular exception). A brand like Yeti nowadays manufactures extremely lightweight down jackets combining high protection with breathability. In short, sportswear today is often not worn for the practice of sport. Sneakers and hoodies have even invaded the more informal workplaces. Although the name or products of some fashion brands like Prada Sport suggest an athletic functionality, the garments can only conceptually be considered sportswear. These are clothes that use the models and innovations—one could say, the aura—of sportswear.

As a result of increasing professionalism, athletes have searched for multiple ways to enhance their performance. One way to achieve this is to find better clothing, which is lighter, aerodynamic, better ventilated, or improves grip. Every little detail helps; for instance, the right fabric for a swimsuit can give the edge of a few milliseconds, the difference between first and second place. When it comes to fabrics, sport brands are the great innovators and many synthetics like nylon and spandex were enthusiastically introduced in sport clothing. Early in the 21st century, this has grown into a fascination with technical gear. New materials with interesting characteristics often

> **Sportswear today is often not worn for the practice of sport. Sneakers and hoodies have even invaded the more informal workspaces.**

result in a hybrid garment that can be used in different social contexts. The growing popularity of cycling has been a catalyst for some practical innovations. Especially pants have been the object of scrutiny. Catering to commuters, as well as riders who crave a casual style of riding, both Rapha and Outlier have created pants that are stylish yet feature a number of functional improvements in the areas of moisture control, durability, and comfort. Technical sportswear brands also use unorthodox cuts and details, with the asymmetrical zipper for jackets becoming an emblematic feature.

New materials with interesting characteristics often result in a hybrid garment which can be used in different social contexts.

Sportswear nowadays displays an interesting dynamic with brands like Aether pushing forward with the development of technical gear like the graphite First Light jacket, while at the same time a strong nostalgic current has established itself in menswear. The retro phenomenon in sport clothing works on different levels. Some manufacturers have rediscovered old fabrics that for some time were considered outdated. In cycling the merino wool shirt with long sleeves has made a comeback after decades of synthetic material being the norm. Merino possesses a number of characteristics like temperature and moisture control, which, combined with a growing interest in natural products, makes for a winning fabric. Cult labels like Giro, which are famous for their revolutionary gear like the Prolight helmet, have been investigating merino in a new line of sober-looking shirts that are perfectly suited for long rides in autumn weather. A strong heritage movement is active in footwear with the simple white sneaker enjoying a comeback. The classic Adidas Stan Smith no longer is used as a shoe for playing tennis but has turned into a conventional retro sneaker that forms a winning combination with jeans. The success of the white leather sneaker has resulted in a number of high-end interpretations like the ongoing A.P.C. x Nike collaborations. The young Italian brand Common Projects made the white sneaker into a high fashion object with their minimal Achilles model, which can only by identified by a golden serial number engraved in the heel.

Nostalgic yearning is perhaps best encapsulated by the success of the preppy look. In its original guise the preppy way of dressing was a crossover of sportswear into casual fashion. Nowadays the style is redolent of another time when people would dress up for social gatherings like poolside parties. Swimwear brands like Orlebar Brown and Vilebrequin largely cater to this nostalgic scenario, where men take a dive in the pool and afterwards fire up the barbecue with a drink in hand. The preppy look can be highly coded and has its own set of handbooks, ranging from the ironic *The Official Preppy Handbook* (1980) to serious historical texts like the vintage *Take Ivy* (1965). One brand from Los Angeles epitomizes this style: Band of Outsiders. Named after a classic Godard film, Band of Outsiders creates a world at the edge of sports like polo, sailing, golf, and tennis. An essential part of the Band of Outsiders collection is the boat shoe in the style of the original Sperry Top-Siders and both brands have indeed collaborated on a number of colorful pairs. Also integral to the Band of Outsiders' aesthetic is the polo shirt with the brand carefully studying vintage polos which it reproduces in countless nostalgic color schemes and designs, often releasing them under the sub-label This Is Not a Polo Shirt. But the sources of inspiration for Band of Outsiders—mainly consisting of artists from the 1960s like Dustin Hoffman or Jean-Pierre Léaud—highlight the crucial difference to mainstream sportswear whose icons are the most successful athletes of the moment.

Mainstream sportswear is a worldwide business that largely drives innovation in fashion, even though Adidas created the Originals line to mine the archives and Puma almost completely turned into a lifestyle brand, recognizing the importance of sportswear in street style. Sportswear maintains a slightly different mode of diffusion compared with other fashion styles. Functional sportswear is mainly bought in megastores, which supply gear for all popular sports. The large sport brands do have a presence in city centers with stores that are exclusively stocked with their own clothing. The flagship stores present luxuriously designed buildings that are often situated in premium spots in order to bestow them with the magnetism of a tourist attraction. Nike World New York is a prime example of this concept. Specialist brands and newcomers will never be able to compete and instead look toward a different model for which the Internet has been successfully utilized. A number of Internet boutiques have made a name for themselves over the years by selling men's clothing by high-end fashion brands. Oki-Ni is one of the pioneering online shops that started to sell more avant-garde sportswear, for instance, the more technical lines of mainstream labels like Nike White Label and the much-coveted sneakers by Lanvin. The growing trend of sport brands collaborating with fashion designers—for instance Adidas with Raf Simons or KZK—is mainly targeted and often sold exclusively at these stores. This structure offers advantages to all parties, with the boutiques selling specialized and fashionable sportswear, the mainstream brands being able to innovate and try out new styles, cuts, or fabrics on a smaller scale—at the same time retaining underground credibility—while the cult brands are given exposure and better distribution.

Sportswear is permanently on the move, the spirit of competition in that sense is as active in fashion as it is in sport itself.

Sportswear is permanently on the move, the spirit of competition in that sense is as active in fashion as it is in sport itself. And, in contrast to formal wear, which has been on a retreat for some decades, the customers of sportswear keep increasing. With the projected life expectancy of people well on the rise, men not only tend to dress more casually, often far into middle age, but the importance of sport in maintaining a good life during old age presents golden opportunities. It is no coincidence that fashion in most futuristic scenarios resembles further evolved athletic garments. Sportswear is here to stay.

OUTLIER

"Our dream is to create a Levi's 501 or Burberry trench coat." Outlier co-founder Abe Burmeister envisioned an iconic garment that would fuse technical innovation with durability. The Brooklyn-based brand presented itself with a pair of pants in an all-round fit—the OG Pants—which still forms the centerpiece of their collection. Its conception was a direct result of certain practical problems facing commuters every day: how to stay dry when riding a bike to work and still look presentable after arrival? The pants Outlier designed quickly became a new standard by combining a modern silhouette with a breathable fabric that could withstand daily stress. The OG Pants freed the wearer of damp days at the office after a rainy ride by drying up in an unprecedented 20 minutes.

In an early phase, the founders decided they did not want Outlier to turn into a niche brand catering to cycling or commuting sportswear. The success of the OG Pants quickly branched out into different garments focusing on durability and innovation while embodying the

Outlier's take on the classic hoodie is stylish and innovative. At first sight the hoodie made of doublefine merino feels like an organic interpretation, although the fabric's breathability and moisture control make it a quintessential Outlier garment. A slightly expanded and buttoned version creates a longer silhouette while introducing a double hood with which the wearer can create a mysterious aura, covering both the head and the face. Already the days of commuting seem like a distant memory. With these garments,

same freedom of movement as biking. The button-down shirt was introduced which combined effortlessly with the pants. This new outfit for a casual style of cycling has become very influential, even impacting the fits of global denim brands. Using unassuming colors while eschewing patterns, the outfit offers an interesting versatility with which one can smoothly move from sport to social situations.

The line of pants has slowly expanded since 2008. The original OG Pants have carefully been given a new fit. The fabrics used by Outlier represent a core value which has been easily transferred to well-known menswear fits like the chino, while the jeans-like slim dungaree is made of a slightly more rugged material. Using the idea of hybrid functionality Outlier now makes pants for different outdoors activities while retaining the possibility of being presentable. Movement through the city is as important as adventures in natural landscapes. So the Climbers pants are slim-fit but feature added stretch points for easy movement in unconventional positions. With a waistband that is higher at the back, the pants are optimized for every activity in which the body is bent, be it climbing or cycling. The same principle applies to the New Way Shorts, classic cut shorts which are ready for daily use during summer days. Yet these shorts double as swimwear which makes them an easy choice for hikes through environments—mountains, coastlines, forests—with unexpected opportunities for a dive.

Outlier is a brand that evolves at a controlled pace. Their line of accessories is limited to a small number of pieces, like a key piece or linen towels, which intuitively fit the overall aesthetic. A more adventurous step has been taken with experimental sweaters and hoodies, which continue their interest in fabrics while adding a futuristic silhouette. The Airspace Transparent Pullover is the stuff of science fiction films. Nearly weightless and made of a three-dimensional mesh, the fabric is breathable yet responds to cool weather by retaining body heat. Both the transparent and merino Airspace blend proved to be very popular and point to an avenue which Outlier could develop further in the coming years.

Outlier enters the domain of cyberpunk elegance. On its website which exclusively sells its clothes, Outlier proudly states: 21st century clothing. They have earned that slogan.

In the German town of Ravensburg you will find a shop with the name Seil Marschall. The old-fashioned lettering on the façade and unassuming display window provide subtle clues as to what drives the most self-effacing of outerwear brands. The shop itself sells a selected range of shoes, kitchenware, scents, and premium denim next to a number of Seil Marschall products of which the canvas backpack is the most representative.

Seil Marschall is a family-owned company which started in 1896 as a maker of ropes (*Seil* means "rope" in German.) How did a manufacturer of these very practical yet unglamorous objects become a classic outerwear brand? One cannot help notice that Ravensburg lies in the vicinity of Lake Constance and the northern foot of the Alps. With rope playing a crucial role in mountain climbing, the manufacturer must have detected a market for outerwear which complements the German love for long

hikes in nature. Nowadays the rope factory and clothing workshop form separate entities and without any obvious marketing, Seil Marschall has grown into a highly esteemed heritage brand.

The brand is a small-scale operation and likes to emphasize one idea: objects should last a lifetime. This only turned into an old-fashioned idea with the rise of mass production and consumerism. Recent developments have signaled a

turnabout with a growing number of people starting to get interested in higher quality goods that are built to last. Seil Marschall fits effortlessly in this trend.

The celebrated backpacks are mainly made of canvas, leather, and wool felt padding together with hemp, brass, and horn details. All garments are handmade in neighboring Bad Waldsee, endowing them with a strong artisanal glamour.

At the moment Seil Marschall is primarily known as a backpack brand. The minimal retro styling has caught the eye of many an outdoor enthusiast. The brand offers a number of models in different sizes, loosely geared towards different activities such as climbing, hunting, and canoeing. The canoepack is the signature piece, featuring the characteristic flap that is fastened with leather straps. The canoepack is available in three sizes including a fashionable mini version in a number of colors. The standard fabric used is waxed cotton twill while premium versions are made of heavy canvas.

Over the years Seil Marschall has slowly entered the market with a line of bags geared at urban activities, for instance gym and courier bags. The largest part of the collection consists of sober outerwear with the same emphasis on durability and craftsmanship. The range of coats presents a limited number of models including an interpretation of

the classic waxed canvas jacket that displays a keen eye for detail, practicable solutions, and a detachable wool loden lining. Perhaps the most rural of coats, the hunting jacket is given a luxury treatment, making it Seil Marschall's most accomplished garment. The weatherproof side of the reversible jacket is made of highly regarded Swiss cotton, while the softer side is made from Scottish tweed. Both sides feature a shooting patch on one shoulder for extra protection from the rifle butt and a number of practical pockets lined with leather straps.

Despite Seil Marschall's modest profile the brand not only found its way into high-end menswear stores but also became an occasional partner in collaborations. A surprising pairing materialized in the 2014 capsule collection by Japanese designer Junya Watanabe who fused his avant-garde ideas with Seil Marschall concepts and fabrics, creating two bags, a vest, and a coat that deconstruct the brand's identity.

Incredibly hard to find is the almost inevitable pairing with romantic designer Frank Leder. In a collection of four backpacks, Leder's signature Deutschleder was used next to Schladminger wool, canvas linen, and waxed cotton. All pieces are accompanied by a vintage object (map, light, blanket, water bottle) raising them to the level of conceptual but wearable art.

SEIL MARSCHALL

ORLEBAR BROWN

With sportswear becoming more technical and understated, the British swimwear brand Orlebar Brown moves against the tide. Futuristic longing is replaced by visions of a sun-drenched life on deserted beaches, yachts mooring at Mediterranean islands, and the hypnotic blue of the swimming pool. A faint glamour of the lost Malibu and Riviera jet-set is channeled by the brand. Founder Adam Brown has often shared the moment he realized there was a pressing need for the Orlebar Brown aesthetic. At a pool with friends he observed how the women all looked great but the men were wearing the standard boxer shorts, briefs, and boardshorts. Brown envisioned a pair of swimming shorts with a stylish look, which could be worn in different social situations, thereby eliminating the need for a change of clothes.

The Orlebar Brown swimming shorts, cut above the knee but longer than a conventional boxer, quickly established itself as the new standard, a timeless garment. In the following years models were introduced in three lengths that use a straightforward cut, invoking the style of the 1950s and early 1960s. Undoubtedly the brand appeared at just the right time with the American television series *Mad Men* creating a longing for the tailored style of said era. This is swimwear from the bygone age of pool parties, the beach lifestyle before the rise of mass tourism. Orlebar Brown shorts are not just well made, they represent an ideal.

The silhouette of Orlebar Brown swimming shorts is instantly recognizable. Contrary to another current trend the brand uses a rich palette of colors which dazzles the eye. The brand's prints are as celebrated as its fits. Prints can be divided into two categories. One consists of a collection of abstract patterns in a classic style redolent of Italian accessories of the 1960s.

The second category can be characterized as ironic, think photographs of beach clichés like the idylls of sunsets, surfing, and tropical beaches. The interest in prints led to one of the most anticipated and natural collaborations in fashion. Italian fashion house Pucci became a household name for the jet-set in the decades Orlebar Brown conjures up by introducing colorful, swirly, almost psychedelic prints. Both brands searched the Pucci archives and rediscovered a number of geometric prints in adventurous color schemes which fit Orlebar Brown almost intuitively. The resulting capsule collection truly forms a milestone in high-end swimwear.

But are swimming shorts enough to carry the Orlebar Brown vision? Life beyond the pool calls for different pastimes: a relaxed game of tennis, the drinking of cocktails, or the preparation of a barbecue. With the overwhelming success of the shorts, the possibility of expanding into a complete line became feasible. One obvious addition is the polo shirt which forms a pillar of the stylish summer outfit. Next to the classic buttoned polo, Orlebar Brown presents a slightly more unconventional version with a buttonless front. In combination with the seldom used toweling fabric this results in a unique interpretation of the polo shirt. Two other staples of summer life are offered with the typical Orlebar Brown touch of simplicity and quality. The footwear collection emphasizes ease of use with flip-flops, sandals, and deck shoes. The sunglasses, again, use classic shapes with a preference for the navigator frame beloved by many an actor (Sean Connery, Steve McQueen) from the era of cool.

The sea can be deceiving. As night falls chilly winds are known to surprise many a sun-tanned body. A collection of linen pants and chinos offer a casual solution to which can be added a selected number of elegant jumpers for evening walks over palm-lined promenades. A more sporty solution is to be found in the combination of extremely comfortable sweatshirts and pants, all with a self-assured flair as if the brand has invented them. With Orlebar Brown the old dream of an endless summer really seems within reach.

JOHN
ELLIOTT + CO

Sweatpants have grown into a casual classic. The athletic pants are versatile and can be easily used for both sports and lounging around the house, often in combination with a shirt or hoodie. The first pair of sweatpants is often attributed to Émile Camuset, founder of French sportswear brand Le Coq Sportif. Over the years, the roomier and warmer sweatpants have become an alternative for the tighter tracksuit pants. The common gray sweatpants are mostly made of a heavy knit cotton and polyester blend. A recent development is the more tailored sweatpants, which often features a slim fit. The young brand John Elliott + Co from Los Angeles has incorporated sweatpants in their line-up of fine-tuned casual clothing with the Lima and Alma offering an upbeat design. The finest model is perhaps the slim-fit Escobar, which was inspired by the warm-up gear of South American soccer players around 1980. The cotton pants come in navy and run tight at the ankles, accentuating the retro silhouette.

Golf has conquered the world at an amazing rate. The sport, which in its modern form was invented in 15th century Scotland, slowly grew into an elite pastime with strict rules. These rules extended to attire with many courses upholding a dress code. It is ex... long, tailored trou... dress trousers with pockets are also accepted. Heritage brand Lyle & Scott offers one of the safest choices in golf trousers. The knitwear brand was established in Scotland in 1874 although ...uced a golf collection in the ...ly the brand introduced ...with the golden eagle. Lyle & Scott modernized its collections over the years with their garments finding a place in youth culture. The current model golf trousers reflect this change, forming an interesting hybrid which looks modern yet will pass the scrutiny of even the strictest golf course. Sporting a puppytooth pattern, the cotton elastane blend will stretch perfectly when taking a swing.

PENFIELD

Every man needs a bag. Modern man likes to carry things, often more than his pockets can bear. Bags can be an essential part of the daily commute or leisure activities. Sport apparel is carried in gym bags while a good hike is almost unthinkable without a comfortable backpack. The backpack with its multifunctional appeal has become one of the enduring models. Manufacturers quickly found out that the bag should have the dimensions to carry a laptop. Many offer special padded compartments that ensure the safety of the device. American outerwear brand Penfield has always been centered on protection while radiating with down-to-earth elegance. These qualities can be found in its bags, which work in urban and country surroundings. The Vance is a small bag that features a laptop compartment and an extra slanted front zipper for quick access. Almost the same size, but slightly boxier, is the Massey which has upper grips and side pockets for water bottles or other outdoor essentials.

RAF SIMONS X ADIDAS

Rubber pool slides are related to the sandal. After the success of the flip-flop a more robust type of sandal was created with a stronger rubber sole that is often ergonomically shaped. The pool slides typically have one wide band which lets the freed heel produce a characteristic ticking sound. The footwear is often worn for hygienic reasons and the thick rubber sole offers plenty of protection against sharp objects. German sports powerhouse Adidas produced its first rubber sandal in 1963.

The Adilette—originally in a navy-blue and white color scheme— became a locker-room favorite. Thanks to its simplicity, the basic shape has undergone few alterations. In his ongoing collaboration with Adidas Belgian designer Raf Simons was given a chance to finally reinterpret the Adilette. The basic shape remains unchanged while important modifications have been made to the colors of the strap and sole. Two-tone and monochrome versions are available, which respectfully modernize this poolside classic.

RAPHA

From the very beginning, cycling has been intertwined with fashion. Riding a bicycle in the city was not only a mode of transportation but also a way to be seen. The clothing of professional racers has known its own evolution before a certain standard was reached of a tight shirt in combination with stretch tights. But cycling has recently seen some interesting changes by becoming more popular in cities, which used to be dominated by cars and public transportation. This new wave of cycling also featured a new, relaxed style which is more casual than sporty. The change was understood by new label Rapha, which formed in 2004 and started to produce a number of stylish retro shirts. The signature item remains the cycling jeans, specially designed for the new generation of fashion conscious riders. The innovative denim is elastic, durable, quick drying and stain resistant. For better visibility, the pants even feature pink binding and the reflective Rapha logo when one rolls up the right leg.

SPERRY TOP-SIDER

Sailing traditionally has its own sense of style. One constant problem is posed by the wet deck with its danger of slippage. The boat shoe must provide grip and water-resistance. What is now known as the boat shoe is a specific model which outgrew its original use. The Sperry Top-Sider is generally considered the first modern boat shoe. It was created by American Paul A. Sperry who was inspired by watching his dog run over ice without slipping. The Top-Sider featured a siping pattern cut in the sole which resulted in a perfect grip. The original shoes also had a white sole which prevented marks on decks. The leather upper was given an oil application to repel water and its look was largely inspired by moccasins with additional leather ropes running through the side of the shoe. Traditionally one wears boat shoes without socks, which results in a casual air. The Top-Sider would transcend its boat shoe function and turn into everyday footwear, which Sperry still offers today in countless versions.

DAN WARD

For centuries men swam naked, until Victorian mores introduced the swimsuit. The less modest swimming trunks have become a ubiquitous garment with the explosion of beach culture in the 20th century. At first swimwear was made of wool but the advent of synthetic material, which dries quickly and keeps its shape over time, revolutionized swimming trunks. Nowadays most swimwear is made of nylon, polyamide, or spandex with a mesh lining. Over the years, different styles, from briefs used in swimming tournaments to knee-length boardshorts, have been introduced. Every model enjoys its moment of popularity although these days styles are worn interchangeably while the classic mid-length swimming shorts continue their comeback. This trend can be found in the collection of Zürich designer Dan Ward who makes high-end swimming trunks in different models. His swimming shorts are very versatile and can be worn both poolside and in informal summer gatherings while the briefs have the usual athletic aura.

NANAMICA
X CHAMPION

The baseball shirt has been worn since the dawn of the sport in the mid-19th century. The flannel shirt was eventually replaced by cotton and synthetics. Thanks to its many styles, with ornate team logos and pinstripes, the baseball shirt became a staple of American everyday wear. Many Major League teams like the New York Yankees still wear the traditional buttoned shirt, which together with broad sleeves and an open collar is now considered the archetypical baseball shirt. American label Champion has produced sportswear since the 1930s when they introduced the hooded sweatshirt. Over the years, the brand gained a presence on fields around the United States with unassuming but well-made gear. With the passing of years, Champion has received heritage status, which has invited a number of collaborations. Arguably the most fruitful of these collaborations is with Japanese outdoors specialists nanamica. Their interpretation of the baseball shirt uses the classic buttoned styling with an original mesh.

ORCIVAL

The long-sleeved cotton shirt has become a basic garment which is often used for layering. Until the rise of technical wear the long sleeve was often used by sportsmen in cold weather. The most famous long-sleeved shirt is the so-called Breton shirt (*marinière* in French). The name references the region on the Atlantic coast where the shirt was traditionally worn by fishermen. In the 19th century, the white cotton shirt with 21 stripes became part of the official Navy uniform. It rose to prominence as the quintessential French garment when it was used in a nautical collection by Coco Chanel. Brigitte Bardot, Pablo Picasso, and Andy Warhol imbued the shirt with new glamour. The long-sleeve shirt nowadays is generic although an authentic marinière is still manufactured in France. One of the suppliers of shirts to the Navy was Orcival, which currently produces high-quality shirts for everyday life. The shirts are still woven in Lyon and made of thick cotton in the different striped color schemes.

YETI

The vest is a sleeveless garment that knows many variants. For example, the early outdoors hunting vest, which featured a number of pockets and gave the hunter better arm movement. The down vest is a modification of the down jacket which—filled with goose feather—became the standard winter jacket. The first appearance of the down vest was during the 1960s when glamorous skier Suzy Chaffee started to wear a brightly colored version. The appeal was obvious: the vest kept the upper body warm while offering movement and ventilation during activity. In the 1980s, the down vest became a popular everyday garment that could be worn over a denim jacket. One of the best manufacturers of down vests is the German company Yeti, which first made a name with its high-quality sleeping bags. Their down vests are extremely light with a medium-sized Cavoc weighing just 115 grams. The Yeti vests are warm but breathable and come in a number of models suited for different seasons, climates, and outdoor activities.

CHRISTOPHER RÆBURN

Swiss legacy brand Victorinox. The eight pieces, produced in the original house of Victorinox founder Karl Elsener, were made by hand and strictly limited to a hundred items each. Most pieces featured locally manufactured nails as a detail. Since their release, the garments have become much coveted. Especially the orange-white hoodie, made of Swiss army air-brake parachutes, is considered a sportswear icon. The Remade in Switzerland project took many by surprise and arguably gained much of its fame after the fact. Numerous menswear enthusiasts hope to see a revisit of the concept in the coming years. In 2013 both brands did repeat their collaboration, in a slightly different way, with the Festival Ready project. With a unique mix of humor and functionality, the range used a bright camouflage pattern for eleven music festival essentials, including a poncho, a tent for two persons, and a Swiss army knife.

It is sometimes said that sports present a temporary replacement for war. Both worlds intersect in the clothes of the young British designer Christopher Ræburn. His garments are remade from military materials—jackets, sleeping bags, or parachutes—which he praises for being functional and waterproof. As a result Ræburn is always on the lookout for overstock material from different armies around the world. In contrast to fashion designers with an interest in camouflage and military chic, Ræburn completely redesigns the original clothes. During this process, most garments lose their military aspect and are converted into something new. Although Ræburn downplays the original use value of the source material, his collections still play a sly game with military symbols and names (the 2013 spring/summer collection is, for instance, named Deploy/Fight.) Christopher Ræburn is based in London and with the exception of some collaborations, his clothes are made in England.

Because materials and functionality—instead of ideas for a radical new fit—drive his designs, Ræburn is often seen as a pivotal figure who points the way toward a new cycle in fashion that renounces wastefulness. The importance of recycling puts Ræburn far ahead in the field of sustainability, making him a figurehead of environmentally friendly menswear. Collections under his own name often present a casual silhouette with a slightly futuristic aura, as if designed for sports that still have to be invented. The influence of sportswear is even more pronounced in his collaborations. Two collections with Rapha have updated cycling wear for the modern city, with the wind jacket becoming something of a collector's item. For the line of limited edition Fred Perry polos, Ræburn presented a number of adventurous patterns which completely redefined the classic garment. Two Moncler R Future Heritage collections have centered on mountaineering and presented a highly technical and lightweight look that is both protective and comfortable at high altitudes. As hybrids of military clothing and sportswear, these multifunctional pieces can be easily adapted to different outfits.

Ræburn's most celebrated collaboration was presented in 2011 with the Re-made in Switzerland collection for the

What does the future hold for this exciting designer? Until now Christopher Ræburn has utilized a large number of small scale collaborations to try out new ideas. Meanwhile his flagship collection has developed a hybrid of sportswear and outerwear that characterizes much of early 21st century menswear. Some observers have wondered if any serious expansion of his collections will result in a break with the fundamental Re-Made concept of recycling military fabrics. Indeed, recent collections have seen the increasing use of Cool Wool. The merino knit developed by The Woolmark Company is known for being lightweight, elastic, and breathable, making it a perfect match for the Ræburn style, while offering an exciting contrast between organic and synthetic materials.

K-WAY

For many men the windbreaker is their most used jacket. The windbreaker is thin, light, and protects the wearer from wind and sudden rain. Most current models are made of synthetic materials, which give the jacket a slightly sporty look. The name windbreaker was once used for a gabardine jacket by John Rissman although it eventually grew into a generic name. These days most windbreakers feature a hood and can sometimes be completely folded into a zipped pocket. This packable feature is often attributed to Leon Claude Duhamel who in 1965 witnessed Parisians running through a shower and came up with a lightweight nylon solution. His brand K-Way went on to specialize in different types of affordable pac-a-macs. The two original models are still available in many colors. The Leon 2.0 is a half-zip with a pouch pocket at the front into which the jacket can be packed. The Claude 2.0 is a full-zip model. Both models are also made in 3.0 versions, which are ventilated and made of improved nylon.

SUPERGA

The canvas shoe is a sneaker with a long history. It was originally developed as a beach shoe in the early 19th century by the Liverpool Rubber Company. In Great Britain the shoe, made of a rubber sole and canvas upper, was given the nickname plimsoll. An American interpretation was introduced in 1917 by Converse. The basketball player Chuck Taylor helped improve the shoe which was named All Stars. For decades, the canvas shoe was used for indoor sports. Eventually the shoe lost its edge, only to gain a second life as casual wear. Another important version was introduced in Italy when Walter Martiny started to produce rubber-soled shoes as Superga. His 2750 model using a vulcanized sole became a classic. The 2750 is still available in a number of colors although the white version possesses a timeless appeal. The slightly later 2950 model has the same minimal look but uses a slimmer natural rubber sole. Both canvas shoes are classics which can be effortlessly combined with different outfits.

GIRO

Before the age of technical fabrics, cyclists often wore shirts made of merino wool. The characteristics of the material make sense as a sports fabric: it protects against cold but is breathable; transpiration is easily vaporized while it is also water repellent. With a growing interest in the history of sportswear, the merino shirt has made a comeback, especially in its long-sleeved version, which is preferred by cyclists who hit the road in colder weather. Many brands offer merino shirts in the retro colors of legendary teams. But more modern and discreet models do exist. California-based Giro, which since 1985 manufactures all sorts of cycling gear like the revolutionary Prolight helmet, offers some understated models. The LS Ride Jersey has the typical tight silhouette cyclists like. The shirt has a full zip and rear cargo pockets, and can maintain a perfect body temperature. An urban take is the Ride Crew ¾, which has a looser fit in a merino–polyester blend for even better performance.

VILEBREQUIN

During summer days, Bermuda shorts are omnipresent. The origin of the Bermuda shorts does not actually lie in the island group. Like the related cargo pants it has military roots. The short pants was standard wear for British soldiers when stationed in tropical areas. The trousers did eventually find their name on Bermuda where they were used by civilians. The Bermuda shorts gained popularity as holiday attire with bright colors and exotic designs. A more dressed-up version turned into a casual basic, which is often combined with a polo shirt. The Bermuda shorts would also become synonymous with the Moorea, a longer model of swimming trunks. One of the pioneers of this style was Fred Prysquel who in 1971, inspired by surfers, came up with a design for longer swimming trunks. He founded the brand Vilebrequin and his Moorea turned out to be a runaway success in Saint Tropez. Vilebrequin still sells the Moorea in many editions next to a small number of conventional Bermuda shorts.

HERITAGE

HERITAGE
CLOTHING

LOCK, STOCK, AND BARREL

NOWADAYS, MOST MEN NEED TO CONTENT THEMSELVES WITH CONQUERING MOUNTAINS OF PAPERWORK RATHER THAN CLIMBING REAL PEAKS. MUCH OF TODAY'S MENSWEAR, HOWEVER, INCREASINGLY ASPIRES TO THE AUTHENTICITY THAT DEFINED THE GOLDEN AGE OF MEN'S FASHION—WHEN CLOTHING TOLD STORIES OF DARING ADVENTURES.

by
JOSH SIMS

In Japan, Nick Clements notes, they call it "dad style." It has also been referred to as "revival" style, or "heritage" style. None of these terms sound especially complimentary, but they are apt summaries of what draws a man toward a particular clothing aesthetic—one, in fact, which has all the in-crowd knowingness of a sartorial subculture akin to that of mods or Teddy Boys, albeit without the underpinning shared love of a certain type of music.

Rather, what fans of heritage style are perhaps most drawn to is the authenticity that the many clothing brands and manufacturing companies which fall under this wide umbrella term are founded in, even if many of them have little authenticity in themselves, having been established only in more recent years. But what they all at least aspire to—even those that lack much history—is a respect for the menswear of the past, by which most probably mean after the early 1900s and before the 1960s.

This, after all, was the golden age of menswear, during which its canon was formed—all of those iconic garments that have come to form the basis of the entire men's casual wardrobe, some of them originating with a single maker, all of them endlessly copied ever since. "Heritage" says it all in its appreciation of both those brands and those styles of clothing that have a long past.

But "dad style"? Clements is the founder and editor of *Men's Style,* arguably the leading journal of the heritage and revival style, as likely to be found in the right kind of menswear store as in a newsagents. A photographer by trade, he began shooting this burgeoning subculture before it really had a name. But, as a middle-aged man, he liked what he saw. "There's a reason why revival clothing is so appealing: it works, it's so comfortable, and it's not childish. That's why the Japanese call it 'dad style.' It's not being a 50-year-old dressed as a 15-year-old. It's claiming an area of style that, thankfully, has nothing to do with fashion trends."

Indeed, heritage style looks to the past not only because, as its exponents will vouchsafe, the clothes are so timeless, operating at a level that is supra-fashion—some of the founding makers will be well known to many but many of the modern makers will be known to just a few—but because period designs tend to be highly functional, even excessively so given most 21st century men's actual needs.

"That's a very male thing—we just love over-specced things that go on and on," says Hitoshi Tsujimoto, the founder of Real McCoy's, one of the most eminent of the new heritage brands, specializing in both reproductions and gently improved versions of menswear classics. "We're not really going to go down 300 m under the water, even if our watches can. Professional cameras, four-wheel drive cars—they're all a bit of dreaming for men. Most of it is so tough it will outlast us. Still, at least that way we're making good presents for our sons one day. Well, it's a good excuse anyway …"

Tell-tale characteristics of heritage pieces might include a high prevalence of reinforced seams and pockets, for example, of easy fits—it is rare to find a pair of pants, for instance, that is tight or has a low rise—and of hardwearing fabrics the likes of leather, duck, chambray, cotton drill, and, above all, denim. These are not only fabrics that one can live in, actively, without fear that they cannot take the abuse, they are fabrics that actually get better the older they get. Certainly it is perhaps a faux pas in heritage dressing to look too new—the pleasure in the clothing is in part that each item bears the marks of the personal journey it has gone on with its wearer. That said, don't expect the true follower of heritage menswear to buy into pre-worn garments—such are considered deeply suspect—unless those garments happen to be vintage originals of the kind so inspiring to heritage brand designers, for which, of course, much kudos is won. If that sounds cultish, it is.

"The important thing is that this is not just a fashion to these people—often it's a way of life," notes Horst Friedrichs, a photographer who has won a reputation for his documentary approach to charting clothing culture, including denim-heads. "You get a feeling for these cultures. Talk to stylists—by which I mean people who really style themselves—and they're recognizing something shared with others. And when you're dealing with a community brought together by the love of a particular fabric, then of course you meet some very geeky people. Certainly one might say it's odd to be obsessed with one fabric—there's no music to go with it, no cars. But these people absolutely love it, the color, the craft…"

The workmanship certainly is there in heritage style—not least because the market has, until recently, been driven by makers in Japan, with its culturally-ingrained focus on detail and, yes, authenticity, and its perhaps surprising post-World War Two enthusiasm for Americana. But also because—especially with younger heritage brands—one standard they typically all adhere to is ensuring that their products are as well made as the historic originals to which they are paying homage. Those on the outside might wonder

why anyone might pay what can seem an exorbitant amount for, say, a simple gray marl sweatshirt when, superficially at least, the same garment can be had for a fraction of the price.

"Food is a good comparison here," argues Roy Slaper, a leading figure among the breed of artisanal denim makers who have found their niche over the last decade. "To the person who survives on a diet of fast food, the discussion of organic or ethical food is abstract and suspect. He points to the hamburger he likes costing $3 and says only a fool would pay more. But you could get a $15 hamburger on the same street. And our jeans are the $15 hamburger. The machines I use are special. The methods I use are special. The materials I use are special. These aren't even perceivable to the fast-clothing customer."

So, apart from the very particular, what kind of man embraces heritage style? "There are the fighters, the lovers, and the stylists," says Clements, jokingly. "The fighters like revival style because it's a kind of gang; the lovers like it because they think it's a way of getting the girls; and then there are those who embrace the dandy gene, especially in British culture—though that can also be found elsewhere too now, in Japan of course, and the US, but also Sweden and Germany—and love it for the look."

In other words, heritage style also appeals to a boyish love of dressing up—although not in the sense of putting on one's finest suit. It is for this reason maybe that many of its fans truly are devoted, adhering to their style not only regardless of the changes of fashion, but also the changes of season. The heritage dresser who favors heavy denims, engineer's boots, white cap-sleeved t-shirts

and a biker jacket is likely to wear the same whatever the weather.

There are limits to this appreciation for the old-time feeling, of course. "It's why an old Rolex can just feel better than a new one, but you don't want a pocket watch, why an old Mercedes has a certain essence to it, but you don't want a horse and cart," says Tsujimoto. And there is the risk of one's wardrobe looking more akin to costume than to everyday, tough menswear. "You can overdo it. You become a pastiche of a pastiche of a pastiche," as Clements warns. "There are times when I've looked like a lost extra from a period movie, which for some people is perhaps a way of saying 'leave me alone' even while attracting attention to yourself."

But, if a psychologist were ever to unpick the deeper appeal of wearing this kind of self-imposed uniform, they might find that it rests, too, in these clothes being decidedly masculine, sometimes even a bit macho—hinting as many do, and often not so subtly, to some of the 19th and 20th centuries' most dominant male archetypes: the cowboy, the industrial laborer, the soldier, the hunter, and the mountaineer. These real men didn't change their dress just because the sun was out.

The times today are very different. "I loved all that Boys' Own stuff out of the 1950s and these clothes are wrapped up in the same sense of history. That spirit of adventure was and is inspiring," as the vintage clothing obsessive and designer Nigel Cabourn puts it. "There's not much happening that inspiring in the same way now is there? You don't climb Everest anymore. You go up by helicopter."

In these times most men spend their working days behind a desk, moving information around a computer, so the appeal of those clothes worn during a period when men were more obviously out there and active in the world—doing, rather than processing—should be obvious. Just ask that guy in the deck jacket, cuffed carpenter pants, and old work boots.

> "Heritage" says it all in its appreciation of both those brands and those styles of clothing that have a long past.

> "There's a reason why revival clothing is so appealing: it works, it's so comfortable, and it's not childish. That's why the Japanese call it 'dad style.'"

FILSON

In the summer of 1896 gold was found at the confluence of the Yukon and Klondike rivers in the northwest of Canada, close to the Alaskan border. Due to the remoteness of the area, it took months for the news to finally reach the towns in the Pacific Northwest. One of these towns was Seattle.

More than a century before it became known for the nineties grunge explosion and the Seahawks, the city was a working-class town with a strong lumber industry and vicious labor conflicts. This changed rapidly after the discovery of gold and the mass migration to the region that started what's now known as the Klondike Gold Rush. Seattle became the main supply point for tens of thousands of people trekking northwards to seek their fortune. That very few of

them actually returned with gold did not seem to stop anyone.

One of the men who took an arguably more sensible approach to the gold fever was C.C. Filson, a former railroad conductor who had settled in Seattle in the late nineteenth century. He started what was officially called C.C. Filson's Pioneer Alaska Clothing and Blanket Manufacturers in 1897, right on time to provide the fortune seekers with the goods they needed to weather the cold, rugged climate they would be facing. Besides being able to keep someone warm, it speaks for itself that the construction and quality of these goods needed to be durable if not almost indestructible: temperatures in the Yukon can drop to -30 degrees Celsius in winter, combined with snow and an almost unbearable icy wind. Providing the prospectors with goods that could protect them properly was not a matter of comfort or style, but a matter of life and death in these conditions.

Using his own mill, he produced blankets and clothing from Mackinaw wool, as well as boots and sleeping bags. Often Filson would provide custom-made items, based on his customers' needs and requests. This custom is also reflected? in the lifetime guarantee policy the company upholds until this day.

After only a few years the Gold Rush stopped in its tracks, but Filson was still able to capitalize on its good name and service. The state of Washington depended heavily on the logging and timber industry, which was also in need of clothing that had to live up to a high standard of toughness and durability. In this era one of the staples of the brand was created— the Filson Cruiser. The 100 percent wool jacket was made to provide warmth, protection from the ever-present rain in the area, and plenty of storage room. To this day the Cruiser remains a best seller and one of their signature items.

From these early days onward, the small local company grew to national fame, providing outdoorsmen with everything they could possibly need all across the USA and Canada. By the 1960s, the Filson family had built up the brand to a household name in the Western hemisphere.

A change in the company came in 1981, when Stan Kohls acquired the company. Formerly a maker of skiwear, Kohls expanded the product line but was adamant to keep the quality and authenticity Filson was known for. For example, Velcro had been around since the late fifties, but he refused to incorporate it in the company's products. Anyone who grew up in the eighties (and experienced Velcro's omnipresence at the time firsthand) can probably attest to the fact that this was a fairly radical choice to make.

Besides being a brand that was primarily focused on functionality, Filson moved in and out of fashion over the last few decades. The rugged, quintessential American aesthetic was adapted by anyone from the late sixties Laurel Canyon country rock/folk scene to the aforementioned Seattle grunge explosion in the nineties, to the more recent revival of heritage and workwear fueled by bloggers and urban outdoorsmen worldwide.

Filson embraced this latest renaissance completely. Besides expanding their product line even more to include things like watches and leisurewear, a defining example of this is the amount of collaborations the brand released in the past few years. A collection with Levi's was released in 2010, combining two classic giants of American clothing into an almost defining point in the heritage revival. More followed soon after: a collection of shoes with Vans, camera bags with photography cooperative Magnum and even bicycles and watches made by Detroit-based manufacturer Shinola.

Even after more than 12 decades, Filson as a company proves to be as resilient and long lasting as their products.

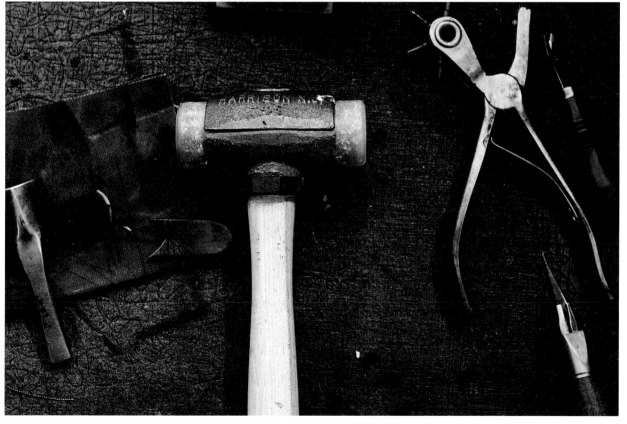

INDIGOFERA

Since 1990 denim has undergone a revolution—the original styles and ways of making have been revisited, first by the Japanese masters, then by the American independents, and latterly in more unexpected quarters, by small companies in Thailand and China. But few can have not noticed that Sweden has undergone its own reappraisal of the blue stuff—and alongside the likes of Nudie, probably Sweden's best-known denim brand, is Indigofera, founded by Mats Andersson and Johan Soderlund and named after the plant from which indigo dye is derived. That attachment to the very source of the fascination (for many) with denim is a statement of intent: if other Swedish denim labels have been more fashion-conscious, Indigofera is true to denim's roots in tough, timeless workwear.

The company brought out its first collection in 2009, after two years of hard work. Both founders quit their day jobs to commit full time to the new brand, but in a sense Indigofera was a question of coming full circle; Andersson and friends—notably the founders of Swedish fashion brands Acne and Cheap Monday—had been trading selvedge denim as long ago as the early 1990s, while Andersson also worked for a time as the commercial director for Levi's Red and Levi's Vintage Clothing.

But why yet another denim label? Andersson has said that the duo's intention was always "not to do what everyone else is doing—from how you approach each piece, the fabric, how it's seen in the marketplace and—in doing so—stand out from the 'pants in denim' thing. We get an idea of creating a certain kind of [denim] fabric and that leads us down, deeper into the process of constructing a pair of jeans."

And while Indigofera also offers shirts, over-shirts, jackets, and even Norwegian-made blankets—inspired by the fact that drivers in Sweden typically carry one with them in the car lest they break down in the snow—it is very much about the denim fabric, sourcing it from mills all over the world in order to find those that are more distinctive. They like "a signature type of fabric, asking ourselves whether we can make a fabric and style of fabrics that people recognize," as Andersson has put it. One such fabric might include, for example, its "gunpowder black" denim, named for the smell it has during dyeing and notable for the white hairline cracks the fabric develops as it is broken in.

Indeed, they launched with a splash: with just 38 pairs of their Clint model (the fit would become the label's staple) made from 16 oz denim that was rope-dyed from natural indigo. That fact alone gave each pair a €1,000 price tag. Fortunately the brand became considerably more accessible thereafter.

Of course, only a committed denim-head might notice the fabric in the first place, and then, as Indigofera's founders have noted, not everyone is going to like it. Indeed, they have pointed out that they often have to offer certain, more unusual denims season after season before they take off. Not that Indigofera is scared to buck even denim-head expectations either—its products are made in Portugal, for example, not a country known for its denim appreciation, and its jeans come not with the traditional chain-stitched hem, but with a running stitch. Why? Simply because that kind of stitch is stronger and less likely to come undone. Tradition should not hamper progress, Indigofera seems to suggest.

HANSEN

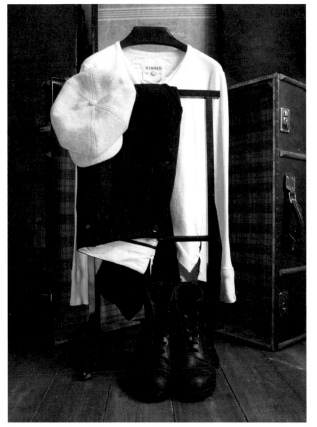

Sometimes an eclectic background can give a new venture a new vision. Perhaps this is what happened with Danish brand Hansen, founded by duo Aase Helena Hansen and Per Chrois, the former with a background in photography and jewelry-making—as well as womenswear design—the latter with a background in film and TV production. The company was launched in 2010—with help from a grant from the Statens Kunstfond, the Danish arts foundation—to provide what Aase Hansen has described as "simple, honest, and democratic design for everyday life—clothing made with a sense of longevity in mind. We craft earnest pieces that cross seasonal boundaries and age handsomely."

This is certainly reflected in the menswear, inspired as it is by a blend of workwear and easy tailoring: crisp, collarless, over-the-head shirts, double-faced indigo work shirts, soft striped henleys, pin-striped waistcoats, and unstructured jackets. Key pieces might be its tie-waisted trousers and matching blazer in denim from the esteemed Japanese Nihon Menpu mill (it is, as Hansen calls it, "unconventional suiting"). Details are key—a men's melton wool jacket might come with shoulders hand-embroidered, for example, in a style that is characteristically Norse (to those who know). A cardigan might be in a typically Norwegian

pattern called hardanger, which is complex to knit. A shirt might come with cat's eye buttons and its cuffs lined with a contrast vintage fabric.

Indeed, fabrics are sourced in Italy, England (especially deadstock ones, which give the garments they're used for a unique appeal), and locally in Scandinavia—especially more unusual materials the likes of elk hide, or muskox wool, which is hand-selected from a supplier in Greenland (a Danish territory) and then spun in Denmark. The result is a sweater which is incredibly warm, but also very soft. Certainly the region's natural and industrial landscape clearly informs the brand's modernistic design. Hansen calls it a reflection of her "longing for the ruggedness of the Norwegian west coast"—she is, in fact, of Norwegian-Swedish parentage, despite being based in Copenhagen. "I'm inspired by the harsh climate."

Yet Hansen's clothing reflects an aesthetic perhaps as much at home in the early 20th century as today—old books and photography from that earlier period have been one key source of inspiration and each collection is pulled together in what might be called an old-fashioned way: by draping and pinning fabrics on a dummy and creating a design and pattern on paper only later. Yet the founders have said they are not enthusiastic about being called a "heritage" brand. "I am very much influenced by the past," says Hansen. "But the word 'heritage' became very fashionable and perhaps lost its meaning or value. We have Scandinavian culture, traditions, and aesthetics in mind when designing [but] our fits and silhouettes are contemporary. Basically we call what we do 'clothing.'"

That is also a reflection of Aase Hansen's determination that her collections not be prescriptive. Indeed, she sees her designs as being versatile, able to be dressed up or down as suits the needs of modern life. And layered up or down as the maybe harsh climate requires, too. Perhaps Hansen's own, rather "poetic" statement on what it is about is the best summation of just how Hansen's surroundings in general shape what each of its collection ultimately becomes: "The sandy seas lined by craggy fjords. Veiled skies ruptured by the sweeping winds of the North. A demure wooden house stands astutely in the adjacent town. Its five industrious floors lit up dimly, keeping the weathered outdoors at bay."

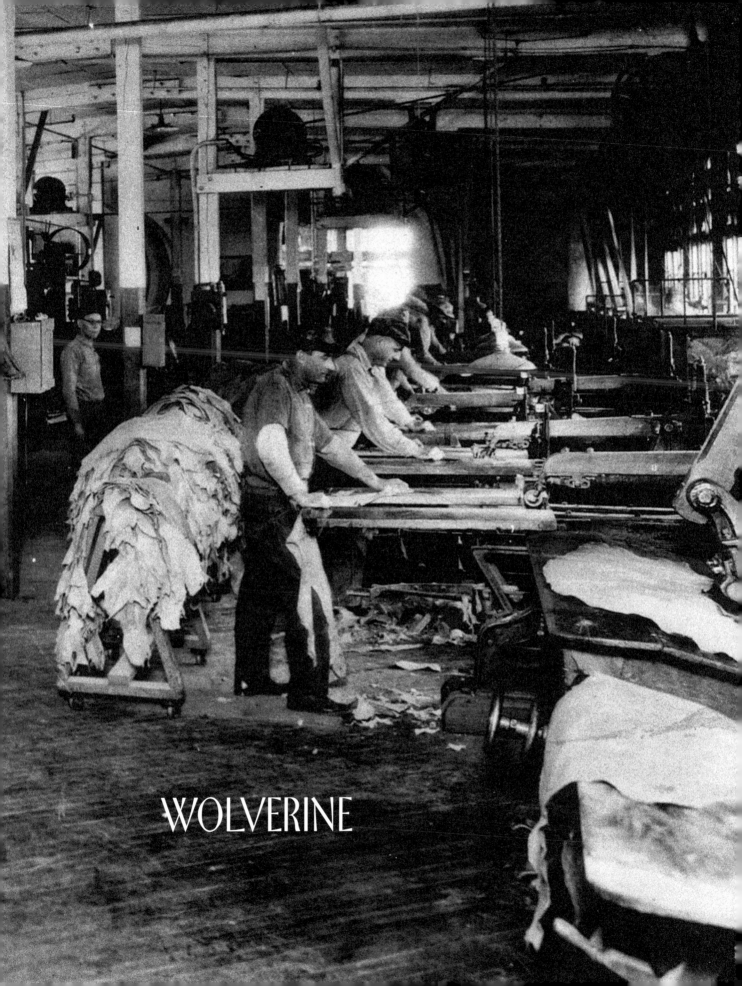

WOLVERINE

Even though the Wolverine company was officially founded in 1883, its history can be traced back as far as Prussia in the early nineteenth century. After fighting in the Napoleonic Wars, Valentin Krause returned to his home country and started a tannery. His son Henry was brought into the family business and learned the trade from his father before following the lead of many others at the time and making the trek westward to America.

Henry settled in Ann Arbor, Michigan. Inspired by the gristmill of the town's founder John Allen and many other mills started by fellow immigrants in the surrounding area, Henry used the lessons he learned in his father's company to start his own successful leather tannery.

Keeping the family tradition alive, Henry's son G.A. also grew up immersed in his father's company. Watching the award-winning tannery grow and expand

to a shoe store and boot factory, G.A. eventually partnered with his uncle Fred Hirth to start the Hirth-Krause Company in 1883. Initially offering wholesale leather goods and supplies, the start of this company turned out to be the official beginning of Wolverine.

Eighteen years later G.A. Krause set his sights on the small Michigan town of Rockford, establishing a power company to provide the town with electricity throughout the day. Following this achievement, G.A. and his sons opened a shoe factory on the banks of the Rogue River, producing 300 pairs of work shoes daily and eventually selling them under the "Wolverine" brand name.

When production grew, it made sense for the company to be able to produce their own leather and in 1908 the Wolverine Tanning Company was established. Years of research went into perfecting the process of tanning Shell Cordovan horsehide—a tough but long-wearing leather. Because of this, the company was able to produce such a high-quality product that survival was guaranteed, even with the Great Depression coming up. Wolverine managed to keep the factories running all the way through the thirties.

In the following two decades, Wolverine moved away from horsehide leather for two reasons. First of all, it signed a contract with the US military to develop pigskin gloves, creating their own patented line of machines to optimize the skinning process.

Secondly, with the tractor and car becoming more common in daily life, there were simply a lot fewer horses around. These reasons forced the company to be creative and find new ways to use the softer pigskin leather, and the need to broaden its horizons led to another success story when the company created a soft, casual shoe made of a newly developed suede leather—the Hush Puppies brand was born.

Introduced when post-war suburbia was growing in the US, it turned out to be the perfect shoe for a new generation. During the sixties and seventies, one-in-ten American males owned a pair of Hush Puppies, according to brand lore. The crepe sole on the shoes even apparently saved Rolling Stones guitarist Keith Richards from electrocution when his guitar and an ungrounded microphone made contact. Like many stories about the man from that era, this might well be just an urban legend.

Even after a hundred years of business, Wolverine never rested on its laurels toward the end of the twentieth century. Besides still producing its signature work boots and Hush Puppies, the company expanded by acquiring the license to produce industrial footwear for Caterpillar. In addition, they acquired a wide range of smaller shoe producers, including some American classics such as Sebago, Sperry Top-Sider, Keds, and Saucony. They also hold the license to produce footwear under the Harley Davidson brand name.

MACKINTOSH

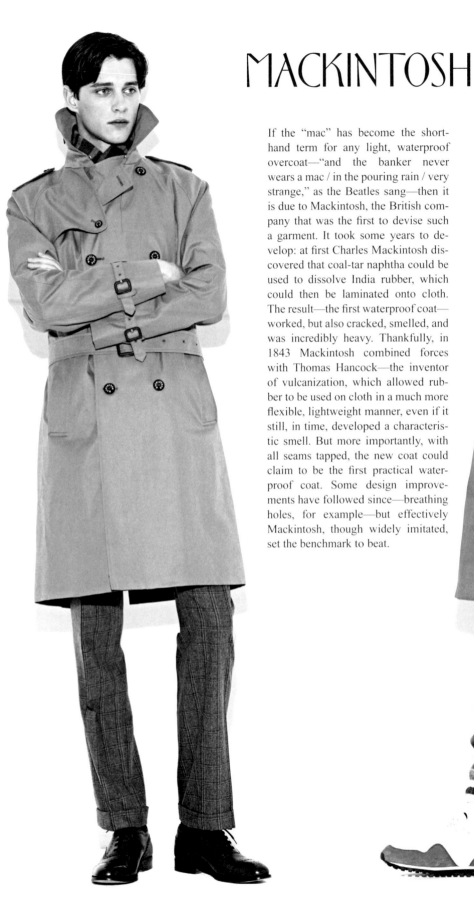

If the "mac" has become the short-hand term for any light, waterproof overcoat—"and the banker never wears a mac / in the pouring rain / very strange," as the Beatles sang—then it is due to Mackintosh, the British company that was the first to devise such a garment. It took some years to develop: at first Charles Mackintosh discovered that coal-tar naphtha could be used to dissolve India rubber, which could then be laminated onto cloth. The result—the first waterproof coat—worked, but also cracked, smelled, and was incredibly heavy. Thankfully, in 1843 Mackintosh combined forces with Thomas Hancock—the inventor of vulcanization, which allowed rubber to be used on cloth in a much more flexible, lightweight manner, even if it still, in time, developed a characteristic smell. But more importantly, with all seams tapped, the new coat could claim to be the first practical waterproof coat. Some design improvements have followed since—breathing holes, for example—but effectively Mackintosh, though widely imitated, set the benchmark to beat.

PENDLETON

Picture the classic lumberjack style of the American Mid-West and chances are it will be woolen and plaid. Such was the style developed at the turn of the 20th century by US manufacturer Pendleton. Indeed, although a specialist cold-weather work garment—worn effectively as a jacket—by the 1960s it had become a recognizable fashion style in its own right: surfers used them to keep warm once out of the water, for example, and The Beach Boys were once known as The Pendletones in homage to the shirt they all wore. What made it distinct from other wool shirts, however, was Pendleton's many check designs, rather than the block colors typically available. That made them akin to picnic blankets—indeed, the company, established in Oregon in 1889, started out making blankets of equally bold designs inspired by local Native Americans' preference for strong colors and jacquard patterns. In fact, Pendleton would end up selling blankets to the local Native Americans. Their picnics were never the same again.

SCHOTT NYC

Ever wondered who was responsible for putting a zipper on your jacket to close it? Or who was responsible for the practical design of that motorcycle jacket you own? That would be Irving Schott, who started his own company manufacturing jackets in 1913 on New York's Lower East Side.

Irving and his brother Jack were the sons of Russian immigrants who came to the United States looking to build a future in the late nineteenth century. The brothers started out making raincoats, which they would sell door to door around the city. Convinced his name would sound "too Jewish" for his customers, he initially decided to name his jackets after his favorite brand of cigars—the Perfecto.

After being introduced by a family friend to Harley Davidson Motorcycles, which were just becoming more widely available after the First World War, Irving

started to develop a jacket that would cater to the growing group of bike enthusiasts.

Riding a motorcycle obviously needs more protection than any other type of vehicle and prior to Schott no wool jacket was able to provide adequate protection against the wind while riding at high speeds. The leather jackets that were available did not provide enough comfort and flexibility for the bike's riding position.

Schott made some revolutionary adjustments—first of all the zipper. While the modern zipper first came on the market in 1913, it was mostly just confined to military use because of high costs. When its use became more widespread, the prices went down and Schott realized he could use the new technology on consumer jackets. The use of the zipper and the diagonal placement on the jacket solved the main problem for motorcycle riders—the piercing wind.

Because the design of the jacket was purely functional, it looked fairly out of place at the time and it took a good two decades before the jacket really cemented its place in the modern pop cultural lexicon. That was the moment Marlon Brando's 1953 film *The Wild One* came out. Brando plays Johnny, the leader of the Black Rebels Motorcycle Club terrorizing a small California town. Wearing his snug black Perfecto jacket he is the ultimate version of rebel cool, inspiring generations of actors, rock stars, and artists. Interestingly enough, sales actually went down during this period due to schools around the US

introducing a ban on the jacket because of the hoodlum image it projected.

A similar sudden explosion of popularity came a few years later when Peter Fonda wore a Café Racer style Schott jacket in counter-culture classic *Easy Rider*. The snug leather jacket with the stand-up collar that Fonda's character wore throughout the road movie became one of the company's most popular styles. The light-brown suede jacket with the western-style fringes that co-star Dennis Hopper wears throughout the film is also made by Schott.

Besides the classic Perfecto Motorcycle jacket, Schott became well known in a completely different field too—the military. When the US got involved in the Second World War after the attack on Pearl Harbor, the company was asked to develop a "bomber" jacket for the Air Force fighting in the battlegrounds

of Europe and the Pacific. Made from sheepskin leather with wool lining, the jacket was perfect for colder climates. A somewhat more lightweight fighter jacket was designed for pilots flying in warmer climates, most notably worn by the Tuskegee Airmen. For the servicemen on deck Schott produced the classic melton wool pea coats, still a staple in menswear to this day. Founder Irving's son Mel Schott even served in Iwo Jima, receiving a Purple Heart for his service. When he returned after the war, he joined his father in the business.

In the seventies, the Perfecto was adopted again by a whole new generation. Bruce Springsteen wears the jacket on the cover of his classic *Born To Run* album, as do the Ramones on their 1976 debut album. The rebellious spirit of the jacket lives on as does the company, which is still going strong to this day.

GLOVERALL

The duffle coat is a classic menswear item made of duffel, a very thick woolen fabric. The origin of the coat lies in the Belgium town of Duffel although it rose to prominence during the First World War as a British Navy coat. After the Second World War the British company Gloverall purchased large quantities of the surplus coats and started to produce their own version. Gloverall also introduced the characteristic leather loop fastening with Buffalo horn toggles which became a standard element of the parka length coat. The duffle coat was very popular during the 1950s and 1960s in both navy and camel but slowly grew unfashionable in later years. Like many classics, it was rediscovered at the beginning of the 21st century immediately changing the fortunes of Gloverall. The current collection offers a number of interpretations of the classic model, which features the traditional tartan lining, shoulder cape, and hood. The Gloverall duffle is a timeless garment that is still made in England.

STETSON

With regard to men's hats, there is perhaps no name more famous than that of Stetson. John Batterson Stetson was, after all, inventor of the cowboy hat beloved of so many real cow-hands and countless Western movies: with a tall crown to let the air circulate and a brim wide enough to protect the eyes from the sun while also channeling rainwater away from the shoulders, it was a great design. And yet it was the product of a jokey bet. Stetson was on a hunting trip when he demonstrated how he could make a cloth out of fur by wetting, matting, compressing, and heating it, rather than by weaving. He made a hat—which, in 1865, would more officially become the cowboy hat—to demonstrate. But it was his fur felt that would prove most important, since this could be turned to make all manner of warm, naturally breathable, and water-repellant styles of hat, including more everyday trilby, homburg, and pork pie styles.

PIKE BROTHERS

When the weather calls for something more substantial the henley top, a short or long-sleeved collarless pullover shirt with a button opening, is the perfect item to wear. Named after the tops worn by 19th and early 20th-century rowers on the river Thames in the UK—specifically around the town of Henley-on-Thames, hence the name—it appeals to an olde-worlde sensibility, which is why brands the likes of Pike Bros, with its precision re-productions of vintage styles, offer among the best. Established in London in 1930—it was soon specializing in the production of uniforms for the US armed forces—but reborn during the 2000s in Germany, its "utility shirt" is based on a 1954 model and has the same period details, being made from brushed cotton jersey and with cat's eye buttons.

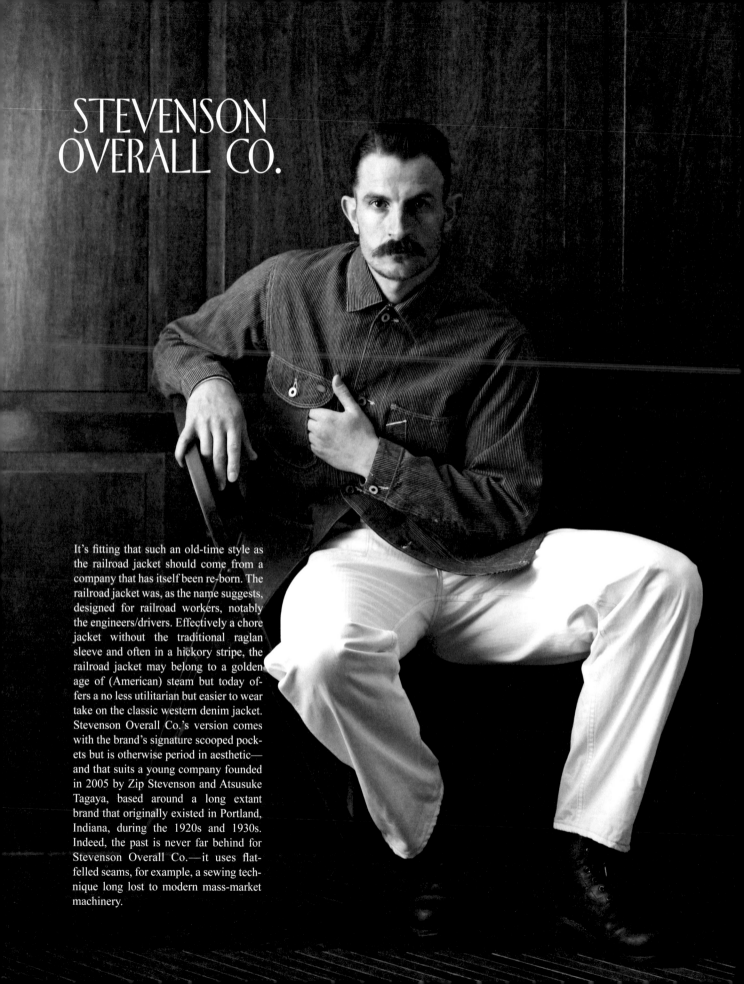

STEVENSON
OVERALL CO.

It's fitting that such an old-time style as the railroad jacket should come from a company that has itself been re-born. The railroad jacket was, as the name suggests, designed for railroad workers, notably the engineers/drivers. Effectively a chore jacket without the traditional raglan sleeve and often in a hickory stripe, the railroad jacket may belong to a golden age of (American) steam but today offers a no less utilitarian but easier to wear take on the classic western denim jacket. Stevenson Overall Co.'s version comes with the brand's signature scooped pockets but is otherwise period in aesthetic—and that suits a young company founded in 2005 by Zip Stevenson and Atsusuke Tagaya, based around a long extant brand that originally existed in Portland, Indiana, during the 1920s and 1930s. Indeed, the past is never far behind for Stevenson Overall Co.—it uses flat-felled seams, for example, a sewing technique long lost to modern mass-market machinery.

RED WING

With its moc toe contrast stitching and its flat white sole, the Red Wing is probably the most distinctive of work boots. Add in the color of its most famous Irish Setter model—a russet brown said to mimic the coat of the dog of the same name—and the Minnesota-based company had a style that looked as at home with jeans on the street as on a building site or hunt. Indeed, the Red Wing company, launched in 1905 by German immigrant Charles Beckman, swiftly won a reputation for making boots built for purpose: from its Brown Chief farmer's boots to its Engineer's boots, which became the template for all biker boots that followed. But it was perhaps its location that ensured Red Wing achieved such utility with its products and not just for its name, borrowed from that of the local Dakota tribe's chief. Rather, the extremes of weather the Minnesota region was subject too—both hot and cold, drought and flood—meant that its boots had to perform in all conditions.

BUZZ RICKSON

Japanese company Buzz Rickson, established in 1993, has not won plaudits for its originality. What it is celebrated for are its reproductions—of quintessential military, work, and sporting garments that have become staples of the male wardrobe. Its MA-1, for example, is an historically accurate copy—right down to the blend of summer-weight nylon for the outer, the use of deadstock Talon zippers and the more streamlined fit—of the flying jacket first issued by the USAF in 1970 to replace the fur-collared B-15. The MA-1 had distinctive design details that Buzz Rickson's version faithfully reproduces: the sleeve pocket, for example, the reversible cut with lining in "rescue orange" and even the chest tabs, which were used to secure radio wires between helmet and cockpit; of course, Buzz Rickson also produces a 1960 B version of the MA-1 in which these tabs were no longer present, because the wires had long since been integrated into the helmet. Buzz Rickson, as with so many Japanese heritage clothing manufacturers, is a master of period accuracy.

L.L. BEAN

Duck boots are the considered dresser's alternative to rubber or Wellington boots. If the latter provide waterproofing to your feet but typically offer a sloppy fit and a sloppy style, the duåck boot combined sturdy outdoor footwear with the added protection of a seamless, wraparound layer of rubber. They speak of days in the wild, hunting and fishing. And, indeed, it was an American company that launched them in order to cater to just such outdoor pursuits and made the style one of its signatures. L.L. Bean was established in 1912 near Freeport, Maine, by the unlikely named Leon Leonwood Bean. He then, as the billion-dollar company does now, sought to devise and provide garments ideal for the sporting life: among its classic garments, alongside the duck boots he designed, are its field coat, chamois shirt, ice carrier bag, and zipper duffle, all of which were introduced between the 1920s and 1940s but are still selling well today.

GITMAN BROS.

The dress shirt might be British, historically-speaking, but the casual shirt—in flannel for winter, in Oxford or cotton cloths for summer—belongs to the US. Small wonder then that, as attire becomes more easy-going, small all-American shirt-makers have enjoyed a renaissance—Gitman being one of the most prominent. Established as a contract manufacturer by Max Gitman in 1932 in Ashland, Pennsylvania—where the factory remains today—it was only in 1978 that it launched its own Gitman Bros label, which later saw the creation of Gitman Vintage for shirts with a more heritage feel, often being made from archive fabrics. Indeed, from a distance, a Gitman Vintage shirt can look like any other button-down shirt—the style for which the brand has become best known. But it's up close that the details are telling: not just the fit, which is neither tight-fitted nor baggy, with a higher armhole and narrower sleeves, but the likes of its double-track stitching, characteristic chalk buttons (including one in the back of the collar), locker loop and three-inch collar—enough to slot three fingers into, according to the test imposed by the Mods to check the collar size.

TELLASON

It once looked as though any denim connoisseur's interest in jeans from the US was all but dead. After all, it was Japanese manufacturers which, over the 1990s, turned again to making jeans as the Americans originally did—before the US denim industry's mass-commercialization in the 1970s and 80s. That is to say, on slow but characterful shuttle looms and with ancient indigo dyeing techniques that give the denim a personality, as well as such traits as selvedge. But, over the early 2000s, such artisanal approaches were embraced

by small American makers again—one of which was Tellason. Established in 2008 by friends Tony Patella and Pete Searson, they have committed to only make their jeans in San Francisco—the birthplace of jeans, of course—using Cone Mills denim, one of the US's last denim makers. They also committed themselves to making their straight, slim styles only in raw denim—it comes very dark, very stiff, and prone to shrinkage, but also, over time, becomes appealingly personalized to the wearer.

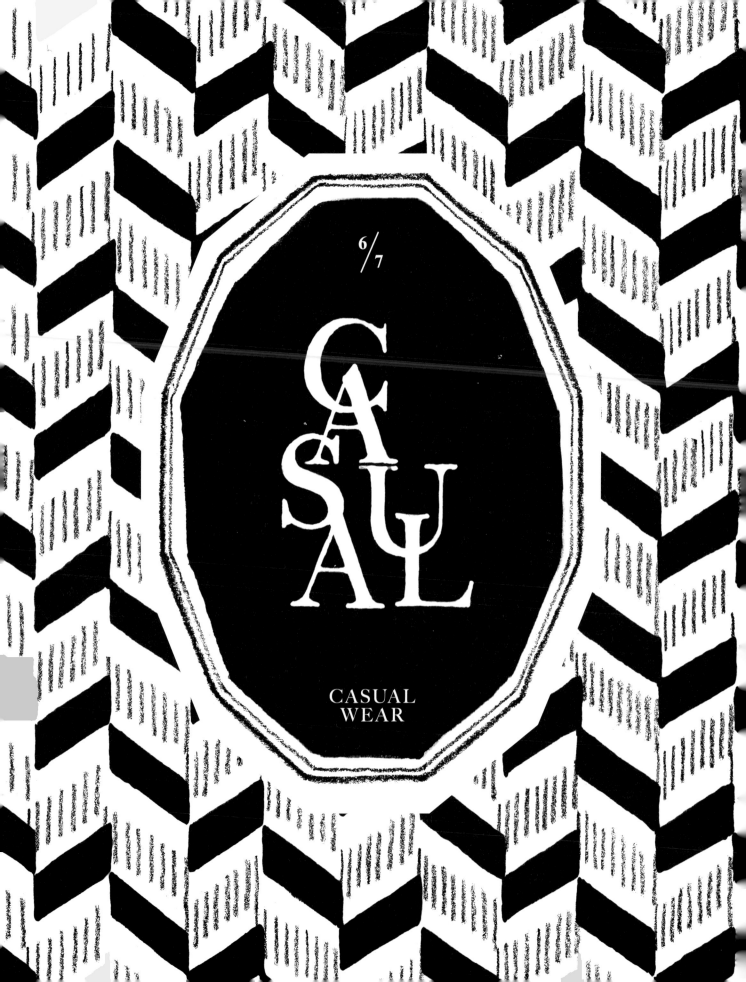

CASUAL

CASUAL
WEAR

THE COMFORT ZONE

TODAY, CASUAL WEAR IN PROFESSIONAL ENVIRONMENTS NO LONGER RAISES ANY EYEBROWS. THE BOUNDARY BETWEEN THE TWO DISPARATE WORLDS "LEISURE" AND "WORK" HAS BEEN BROKEN. MAINTAINING A COMPANY IMAGE IS NO LONGER DONE WITH A SUIT AND TIE.

by
JOSH SIMS

The very idea of casual wear can sound like a misnomer in the 21st century. There was a time when an important element of our working lives was dictated by how we dressed—in terms of meeting employers' expectations, in terms of playing a part to clients and customers. "Casual" was what was worn outside of this environment—in the evenings, at the weekend. That gave birth to the equally odd term "weekend wear" too.

It tended to imply the kind of saggy, comfort-driven clothing in which one might be able to do all the household chores—clothes that were not typically a reflection of one's taste, personality or style but of the practical need to get stuff done, even if that was just laying on the sofa. It also gave birth to that terribly confusing and increasingly redundant idea of "smart casual," neatly, pointlessly, falling between two stalls and, in the end, looking neither smart nor casual. Dress up but don't wear a tie—it is the incarnation of much business dress today in fact.

Thankfully much has changed since the start of the new millennium, in the work place, and in menswear alike. Many if not all forms of employment, for example, no longer insist on a strict dress code, even if some specific garments—jeans, most notably, are still to come in from the cold, sartorially-speaking. For every bank or insurance company that does still impose expectations of smart dress, there are media and creative companies for which anything goes—jeans, indeed, sometimes seem to be mandatory. Casual clothing here does precisely what smart clothing was once believed to do: set the right tone, project a (company) image. Now many companies want to come across as more approachable, personable, relaxed: Dress down and don't wear a tie—ever.

More generally, in menswear the lines between casual and formal wear (or whatever the opposite of casual wear might be considered to be) have broken down, such that many more men no longer make a distinction between their casual and formal wardrobes—unless they are attending one of the key life events, such as a wedding, funeral, or court appearance at which the wearing of strictly formal attire is still the social norm.

In fact, casual clothing is increasingly becoming what formal clothing used to be—the default option, whether at work or not. A century ago, for most men the idea of casual clothing simply did not exist—unless one was a manual laborer of some kind, who was required to wear specialist clothing, one simply wore much the same, mostly tailored clothing, whether at work or play. Even those who dressed most formally for work had only one change of style—toward the more formal, the more special, one's so-called "Sunday Best." And many men who did have manual jobs similarly wore the same clothing in and out of work.

Clothes, after all, were expensive, expected to last many years—and, thanks to a culture of repairing, would be made to last. A man typically did not have the luxury of distinguishing between casual and formal attire. Only the very well-off might dress differently for their holidays or to play a sport. In fact, historically, it was the rigors of sport that played a major role in the introduction of a softness and functionality to a kind of clothing worn outside of work—and even today, outside of the specialist clothing market, technical advances in construction and fabrics are more likely to be explored in casual clothing than formal, the latter tending to regard the traditions of silhouette and noble materials as an important touchstone.

The creation of casual menswear would necessitate a major social change: the "invention" of the teenager. Up until World War II, young men (and women)

> **In menswear the lines between casual and formal wear have broken down, such that many more men no longer make a distinction between their casual and formal wardrobes.**

effectively dressed like their parents the day they packed away their school uniforms: In terms of style, the young adult was merely a version of their older selves to come. But a global conflict in which so many men were torn away from their homes and forced to grow up very quickly, a post-war consumer boom (in the US at least), and a pop cultural renaissance were all factors that generated a seismic shift in the way society was structured: Men typically still in their early to mid-20s returned home changed, more independent-minded, wanting something other than what older generations had had and expected them to have too. They thought differently, danced differently, and, perhaps wanting to escape the restrictions of uniform, wanted to dress differently, too.

The Beat poet Jack Kerouac is a case in point. While he was typically photographed in blazer and tie for official publicity stills, in his personal life he dressed in a new kind of casual way, in rugged, simple, and affordable sportswear and military surplus from the depots that had sprung up across the US: tight black or white t-shirts, plaid work shirts, and PT sweatshirts—Kerouac was a star college athlete—standard issue khakis, cowboy or work boots, bomber jackets and US Navy pea-coats, all thrown on without much regard for how it all looked. His clothes mirrored the other, similarly free-form new arts that Kerouac so loved: bebop, jazz, action painting, automatic writing. Perceptions of hip—to use the terminology of Kerouac's circle, as it defined this new, creative lifestyle of the loose and easy—would henceforth be formed on the street and filter up, not trickle down from further up the social ladder. Kerouac's style—and that of many disaffected men of his generation—may in itself have been basic and unconsidered, but its influence was revolutionary.

What Kerouac wore in breach of the norms would raise no eyebrows

> **While the elegance of a beautifully cut suit is likely to win a man respect for his style, it is in a more creative, essentially casual mode of dress that a man is more likely to be applauded as "cool."**

at all today. Indeed, compared with casual wear nowadays, it might even look a little scruffy. Today's idea of casual wear—precisely because it has become the standard way of dressing, rather than a counter to formal attire—is anything but sloppy. Casual wear today, in fact, represents a new dynamic—that of a hybrid style. Shirting can still be crisp, jackets have lapels, denim can be clean, dark, and smart. There is little about it that could really be considered to mark anyone out as unrespectable, as it once might have just a few generations ago. Indeed, some garments that were once considered the preserve of smart dressing—vests and bench-made shoes, to name just two—have been re-appropriated as part of "casual" dressing. This shift has meant a key change for the formal wardrobe, too. Men are no longer always obliged to wear the standard suit and tie ensemble to work. As a result, they are more likely to wear a suit when socializing—they dress up to go out instead.

This shift has meant that casual today is defined more by the details in men's clothing than by the obvious visual cues and stereotypes of the past. The silhouettes that perhaps once distinguished formal attire are no longer owned by it—a strong shoulder and a clear line, for example, are as much the preserve of casual dressing. Casual clothes fit well—they don't hang off the body. They are perhaps simply more likely to come with a broader color palette, in softer fabrics—cottons, linens, lighter weight wools—and embody what seems like a lack of structure but is often technically complex that is both more naturally form-fitting and comfortable. Shirt collars are more likely to be unlined, a jacket to be free of all the typical padding, while a tie—worn because one

> **Casual wear today, in fact, represents a new dynamic—that of a hybrid style.**

wants to, not because one has to—might be slim and knitted, rather than fat and glossy. It is, in many respects, a much more functional, "go-anywhere" way of dressing. It is a much more modern way of dressing, too.

It has even brought with it a shift in men's style heroes. For every Hollywood star of the golden age who used to be celebrated for his supreme elegance—a Cary Grant or a Gary Cooper, essentially those men who, to quote Irving Berlin, looked like "a million-dollar trooper" in the sharpest of suits—now the names more typically referred to are those of men who, either through their film roles or in their personal lives, know how to dress individually by dressing down. Barely a day passes when a style editorial does not bow down before, for instance, Steve McQueen—a man who, on screen, was often dressed immaculately in conventional terms, as in "The Thomas Crowne Affair," but who was more at ease off screen in a chambray shirt, khakis, and desert boots, clothes that suggested a certain, old-fashioned, outdoorsy masculinity of a kind that, in all reality, most men's urban, nine-to-five lives today only can pretend at.

Indeed, while the elegance of a beautifully cut suit is likely to win a man respect for his style, it is in a more creative, essentially casual mode of dress that a man is more likely to be applauded as "cool." McQueen, in particular, made it a studied part of his public persona—his first wife, Neile Adams, encouraged McQueen to embody it, to make it a central tenet of his screen presence, and it was she who suggested he wear sleeves only to the elbow so that his forearms became the focal point of his sex appeal; note, for example, how in *The Great Escape*, McQueen spent much of his screen time in a blue sweatshirt with sleeves cut off at the elbow. McQueen's son Chad would later define his father's dress sense as "stylish but low-key—his persona was about flying under the radar." Perhaps the ideal definition for men's casual style in the 21st century.

A.P.C.

The understated and minimalistic in menswear can often be uncomfortably close to the dull and uninspiring. But, maybe because it is Parisian—the French stereotypically having an ability to transform the very subtle into the very stylish—that is certainly not the case with A.P.C. or Atelier de Production et de Creation to give it its full name, a name that in itself is direct and functional. And it certainly wasn't the case when the company was founded by Tunisian-born designer Jean Touitou in 1987. At that time its stripped-back aesthetic, a product in part, Touitou has claimed, of growing up in a house full of Swedish design, was a welcome counter to the glitzy global designer names then dominating the fashion scene.

He wasn't being rebellious, the designer has said, "Because what I do isn't so brave." But, in its simple style—clean, dark denim, updated Harrington jackets, fitted sweatshirts, contemporary casual shirts, reefer jackets, desert boots, sophisticated basics, well priced and in good fabrics—it was offering an alternative vision of how to dress. And a singular vision too: "If I were a customer, I would do a survey of the brands that are out there, but why should I look at that if I am doing it [designing] myself?" he has commented. "A baker makes his own bread. He doesn't go to the other bakeries for bread."

It was, ironically perhaps, one of those big designer brands of the 1980s that inspired him. In his mid-twenties then—a would-be student revolutionary in the spirit of '68/'76, having considered and then rejected training as a history teacher, and having spent a year traveling around South America—Touitou fell in with new friends working for Kenzo and liked the designer's more creative approach to business. After years working around the company, Kenzo's partner helped Touitou establish his own record label. When that didn't work out, he returned to Kenzo as its accountant, finally going it alone with A.P.C. To finance this new project, Touitou designed on the side for the likes of Joseph and helped Agnes B with its retail expansion.

Touitou has joked that he needed the money because his A.P.C. designs were "unsellable, because it was so minimalist."

But a clientele for his different style—what Touitou has described as "affordable, trendy, not high fashion, not streetwear, a combination of fabric, cult, cut, price, image, and dopeness"—slowly grew. And slow and relatively small was how he liked it.

Indeed, Touitou has spoken out about A.P.C. and its philosophy of embodying longer-term values, not growth for its own sake—"For many in this business, if they can make something and multiply it by nine, it's like having a shot of heroin in the arm, a kick. I don't get a kick from that [because] at the end of the day the quality will never be there. Same thing with the cutting. It looks like a money hole for them. But if you work hours and wait for the cut to be perfect, it's a game changer. I get off on running the company, making a decent profit, paying people fairly, and having more than a decent life for myself—but that's it." Rather than build an art collection with his money, Touitou opened a school—A.P.E., or Atelier de la Petite Enfance—in response to what he saw as Paris's declining public school system.

It is, perhaps, an unexpected move from this purveyor of a particular type of tasteful cool—"there is a vibe there that isn't said, but it's in the air," as Touitou has described it, apparently finding A.P.C. just as hard to define himself. However A.P.C. might be described, its menswear has won high-profile and diverse fans—from Jarvis Cocker to Kanye West, who collaborated with the company on the creation of entire spin-off collections—who appreciate its "je ne sais quoi" as they say in France.

SLOWEAR

By the reckoning of fast fashion, a model that posits a rapid turnover of very current styles at very affordable, almost disposable prices, Slowear sounds positively old-fashioned, which is one thing a clothing company can ill afford to be. Indeed, the Italian clothing group is, as the name suggests, in no hurry to deliver radical changes of style to keep the pin numbers punching.

"Slowear seemed like the right summation of our philosophy, even if it's an odd word," says co-founder Roberto Compagno whose Venice-based Incotex family clothing business, established by his father, began trading over 50 years ago. "We're against fast fashion in the way the slow food movement is against fast food. That idea was pretty exotic just 10 years ago and a lot of people in the industry thought we were pretty strange guys. Now it's more widely understood."

Certainly, in keeping with a niche market that demands sustainability and cradle-to-grave design in other products, Slowear aims to bring the same in clothing. Much as a growing interest in provenance is being applied to foodstuffs, so, Compagno reckons, it will be to clothing, especially as the fashion consumer's understanding of manufacturing, margins, and build quality improves, in large part thanks to the internet. It's less about who made your trousers than where and how they were made.

The Compagno family business takes an unusual tack. It launched as a uniform maker for the military before specializing in pants, "And over time there was really nothing we couldn't do with pants that we hadn't done," says Compagno, "so we started to apply the same idea to other products." Then there is its approach to design.

Rather than push seasonal collections, it launches new products regularly but only as and when it sees fit, in short, when its technical department—which absorbs five percent of turnover in research and development—has created something new. It has something of a track record in this: among its proprietary fabrics are Chinolino, a cotton/linen blend that retains the breathability of the latter but the softness of the former, and Incochino, a yarn-dyed gabardine with a three-way construction that took five years to develop, as well as Flexwool, IceCotton, and ShadeCashmere.

The company can also lay claim to pioneering garment dyeing—applying dye to a finished garment rather than making it up from dyed fabric—while Slowear's youngest brand RED (for "research e-distribution") is dedicated to exploring the very latest fabric treatments and effects. Look out for its stretch fabrics for men and those using a new, non-GM, organic cotton from Zimbabwe.

"There are plenty of stories of old Italian companies still doing it now as they did decades or centuries ago," says Compagno. "But that's really not us. We use the most technically advanced machinery on the market with the intention of pushing innovation to make the best products. Our thinking is that if you get the fit and proportions right, these are clothes that will still work and still look modern in 50 years."

The irony, perhaps, is that the amount of work going into each garment will be lost on most consumers, in no small part because, superficially at least, the design is unshowy, clean, and contemporary. Each shirt, for instance, is washed three times using a process that does not distress the fabric but gives the shirt that soft, in-built sense of ownership before anyone has worn it. There is very little ornamentation and no logos.

"Consumers now want to take a more personal approach to finding products that are right for them now," says Compagno. "The recession has meant they care less about brand. They want innovation and quality at a reasonable price. Over recent years, fashion almost by definition hasn't looked to quality because there has been no point. The fashion is over before you know it. But that approach is changing. And brands will have to change too."

ZIMMERLI

Too many men overlook their underwear—out of sight, out of mind. Not Johann Jakob Zimmerli. The Swiss entrepreneur's dye house had gone bankrupt when he read about the development of a new, manual, single-needle knitting machine. He sent his wife Pauline to see the machine and she returned trained in the knitting of men's socks—initially the new company makes just 12 pairs a day. Indeed, it is really her drive that pushes the company forward—perhaps fittingly given that the vast majority of men's underwear is still bought for them by women. She helps to pioneer the next technology—a two-needle knitting machine—which allows her to make ribbed fabric undergarments. It is around 1871—and both a family business and the modern underwear industry is born.

Certainly, Zimmerli was modern in its outlook from the start, and for more reasons than its willingness to invest in the latest machinery. Pauline Zimmerli and her descendants understood what most competitors had failed to realize: that underwear is the one area where a customer might invest more in his clothing than perhaps in those garments that actually get seen, because it is one's undergarments with which one has the most intimate relationship.

Firstly, fashion is not so important here, which is why Zimmerli's products—its briefs, boxer shorts, vests, t-shirts and, latterly, polo shirts—tend toward the classical in styling, or "purist" as the company prefers to call it. Many of its garments could have been worn at almost any time since the company's creation—and although the company makes its undergarments in a wide range of prints and colors, black, navy, and grey marl being popular, by far the biggest seller is a suitably purist plain white. Secondly, with underwear being worn next to the skin, comfort is essential, which is why Zimmerli is best known for its ribbed garments, with their close fit and ease of movement, and supposed "ladder-proof" construction.

This is why Zimmerli—which is based in Aarburg, west of Zurich—has traditionally used not only that technology which, for example, makes seams as flat and unobtrusive as possible, or which allows for the elastic waistband in a pair of boxers to be covered with fabric (rather than left exposed as with so many), but only natural fibers too. Merino wool and raw silk, for example, are key—utilizing their in-built performance characteristics of warmth, breathability, washability, and so on.

Cotton is a favorite of course—but Zimmerli sources its cotton only from the West Indies, where the cotton is hand-picked and the long fibers can be spun into especially fine fabrics, with mercerization not only giving them a lustrous sheen but allowing them to wick away moisture more efficiently. Zimmerli's certified Sea Island cotton yarn is so fine that 10,000 meters of it weighs just one gram. The company claims that only the top 0.0004 percent of the world's cotton is good enough to be used. Even with the more technical fabrics—the likes of MicroModal, a specialist, very soft and flexible jersey fabric containing elastane—the origins are natural: MicroModal is made from beechwood cellulose.

Such detailed production does not come cheap—Zimmerli places itself firmly at the luxury end of the market, a position maintained in part by its underwear being selected by costume designers to make appearances in movies the likes of *Rocky, The Matrix, Ray, Walk the Line,* and *Fifty Shades of Grey.* Those white tank tops worn by Hugh Jackman in the Wolverine movies and, iconically, by Bruce Willis in the *Die Hard* franchise? All by Zimmerli. That alone might convince many men the investment is worth it.

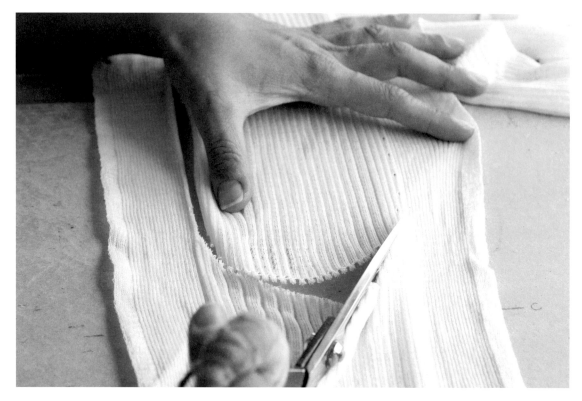

AGNÈS B.

Not quite knitwear to layer, not quite a jacket, the shawl-collared cardigan is the most all-season useful of cardigans—that button-up knitwear first devised by Thomas Brundenell, 7th Earl of Cardigan, during the Crimean War in 1854, both to fend off the evening chills and, it is said, because it could be put on and taken off without messing up his hair. The shawl collar was later borrowed from smoking jackets and became a rugged favorite for the likes of Steve McQueen.

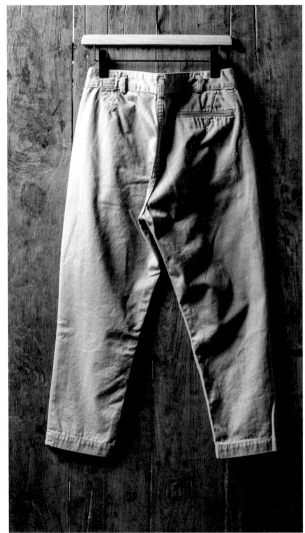

ORSLOW

The crisp, well-tailored chino may have become the default item for every "dress down Friday" but, teamed with a modern blazer, this smarter take on khakis does offer a less formal style when formality is still required. Orslow was established by designer Ichiro Nakatsu in Hyogo, Japan in 2005, taking 19th and 20th century workwear, re-cutting it for a more contemporary fit, and then re-making it in special fabrics using vintage machines.

Its take on the chino cuts it slim for a more tailored look and uses a tough cotton cloth made exclusively for the company, while respecting the detailing that made this originally military garment so utilitarian and hard-wearing, including ticket pocket, jetted rear pockets, reinforced belt-loops, and button fly. Indeed, as the name implies, attention to detail is Orslow's philosophy—slow, as opposed to the rapidity of fast fashion.

CLARKS

As a 1950s ad had it, Clark's desert boot—one of the most copied styles of all time—has "legendary qualities in hot climates." Indeed, shoemaker Nathan Clark was inspired to design it—with its simple split suede, two-eyelet boot construction, and natural crepe, stitched-down sole—when he served in the British Army as part of a West African Brigade. He spotted these "crepe-soled, rough suede boots," as he put it, in Burma (Myanmar) on the feet of off-duty British Eighth Army of-ficers. They had had them made in the Old Bazaar in Cairo. He returned to Clark's, based in Street, Somerset, UK to create an updated version initially considered too radical for most tastes—it found its first success in the US. By the 1960s, designers the likes of Hardy Amies were appreciating the versatility that the soft, hardwearing, boot has retained until today, teaming a pair with a Savile Row suit.

G.H. BASS

The loafer was born of traditional hand-sewn moccasins worn by Native Americans and other indigenous peoples, like the Scandinavian Sami, from whom the Native Americans might have taken the idea. Certainly the idea has traveled: it was an employee of Wilton, Maine-based shoemaker G.H. Bass who discovered the Norwegian variant while on holiday, inspiring the company's first dress loafer in 1936. Bass added a thick sole to make the style sturdier, as well as a vamp saddle with a cutout diamond-patterned slot in which wearers could place a penny, hence the name "penny loafer." Indeed, the Bass Weejun—from "Norwegian"—quickly became the definitive loafer, the choice not only of preppy college students but also the likes of actor James Dean. More upmarket versions come in high-shine, hardwearing cordovan leather, with or without tassels or kiltie fringe, but either way looking as good with denims as with tailoring.

AQUASCUTUM

The story of the mac begins in England in part with John Emery, owner of a menswear shop on London's Regent Street. In 1853, he developed the first waterproof wool, a product he patented and launched under the brand name Aquascutum (Latin for "water shield"), immediately supplying capes, field coats, and a forerunner of the trench coat to troops of all ranks fighting the Crimean War. Later his company would corner the market for supplying the movie industry, with Robert Mitchum, Humphrey Bogart, and Peter Sellers, among others, all wearing the Aquascutum Kingsway trench coat on screen and off. Much about the largely unchanged design—like that from rival Burberry—made it, then and now, an exemplar of military functionality: the epaulettes, the D-ring, originally used to hook on ammunition pouches and other supplies, as well as the protective throat latch, wrist straps, and "rain shield" across the back, channeling water away from the body.

ASPESI

The usefulness of the blazer is perhaps suggested by the sheer diversity of variations created by Aspesi, the menswear label founded in Legnano, Italy by Alberto Aspesi in 1990 (who has been manufacturing since 1969): styles, taking their cue from workwear, in cotton or linen or nylon, buttoning to the neck or, more traditionally, like a suit jacket, unlined, unstructured, quilted, and even hooded. The brand—which conducts extensive fabric research, turning what might be a basic style into a more distinctive piece—makes the most of the blazer's heritage as semi-formal tailoring, able to be dressed up or down as the occasion demands. Indeed, the style originated in a Royal Navy captain's attempt in 1837 to make his crew fit for inspection by Queen Victoria by kitting them out in short, dark, brass-buttoned, reefer-style jackets. The name of his ship? The HMS Blazer.

MYKITA

Sunglasses were first developed for aviators during the late 1920s but, like so many items of military application, quickly found popularity among the wider public—in this case the design-for-purpose shape, tint, weight, and strength, all appealing factors then as now. But sunglasses design has, of course, moved on—high-tech construction, materials, and engineering from companies the likes of Mykita, have ensured that. Established in Berlin, Germany in 2003 by industrial designers Philipp Haffmans and Harald Gottschling, Mykita combines hand-assembly with smart thinking: It devised an origami-inspired, click-together hinge, for example, that does away with the need for soldering or screws, and has pioneered the use of Mylon, a polyamide made using selective laser sintering, which is 40 percent lighter that acetate (a more traditional material the company also works with) and much more durable.

TAMAKI NIIME

Whether to warm up in over winter or to simply wear for a splash of color over the summer, a scarf is an essential accessory—and an opportunity for self-expression. Designer Tamaki Niime is based in Nishiwaki City in Hyogo, Japan, an area known for its banshu-ori, a cotton or wool fabric made with distinctive variations of color and pattern using a signature dyed-yarn weaving technique dating back 200 years. The weaving process—on vintage 1960s' looms Niime inherited—is especially slow in order to create a loose weave and a feathery feel which is actually much stronger than it looks. The fabrics, distinctive too for being intentionally unevenly textured, are then sewn into scarves and shawls, washed, and dried in the sun. Niime underscores the quality of her products, first launched in 2004, by using organic cotton, too.

COMMON PROJECTS

A classic pair of white sneakers—minimal labeling, no loud colors, no high-tech cushioning systems—has been a wardrobe essential since Converse effectively invented the form with its One Star low-top and Jack Purcells, and the likes of Adidas added to it with its Stan Smith model. But a more premium take on the comfortable, ubiquitous style requires a smarter finish—that was the thinking behind Common Projects based in New York, its products made in Italy, and launched by Prathan Poopat and Flavio Girolami in 2004. Its shoes—each model stamped with a gold foil number indicating model and size, but otherwise branding-free—are as monochromatic as the sneakers that inspired them. But while Poopat describes his shoes as functional—akin to "things that do what they're supposed to," as he has put it—they are made in upscale leathers and canvases. These are sneakers for grown-ups.

MOMOTARO

The fabric might have originated in Cambrai, France, but it was the US Navy's use of chambray for its sailors' work shirts during Second World War that really put this tough, lightweight, woven cotton fabric in the spotlight—and which saw a growing appreciation for the way it softens and fades like denim. But, much like denim, Japanese mills have perfected the production both of this traditionally indigo or light-blue material and the construction of the functional, casual shirts it is used to make. Momotaro, for example—established by the Japan Blue Company in Okayama, Japan in 2005—triple-stitches all of the seams on its shirts, the forepart of each sleeve is reinforced, the neck has a throat-latch, the two breast pockets come with pen slots, and the buttons are of the cat's-eye style, as were typically found on the original US Navy models.

MERZ B. SCHWANEN

The sweatshirt might have been an American invention—devised by Bennie Russell for the Russell company of Alabama in 1922 as a tough cotton alternative to the heavy woolen warm-up sweaters then worn by American football players. Since then, the garment—traditionally in an off-white or grey mélange color and improving with each wash—has been made by many companies. But some pay more attention to the original design details: undershirt manufacturer Merz b. Schwanen, founded in 1911 in the Swabian Jura in Germany, for example, makes its "sweater" using rare circular knitting machines in a heavy three-thread cotton fleece, with a one-piece sleeve and traditional ribbed triangle inserts, front and back, at the neck. There are functional details too: at each armpit is another ribbed triangle, allowing for better movement should you ever decide to actually get sweaty in your sweatshirt.

MÜHLBAUER

A family company with a heritage dating back to 1903 might not be expected to have a modern sensibility—especially when it comes to hats, a category of menswear that has been in decline since the 1950s with the advent of central heating, increased car travel, and less formality. But Klaus Mühlbauer, who took over the Vienna-based Mühlbauer from his parents in 2001, sees it as an opportunity for expression—to use traditional, manual hat-making skills such as stiffening, molding, steaming, turning, and blocking, but with a contemporary approach. The result are styles that are more dressed down than up: its narrow-brimmed, low-crowned, pork pie variants with their crumpled aesthetic are the most versatile style, in straw braid for summer—offering sun protection without heating the head—or fur and velvet felts for colder days.

SUNSPEL

When Thomas Hill had his simple idea, he created one of the most iconic garments in the world: the t-shirt. The man behind the British company Sunspel, established 1860, had long been making long-sleeved cotton underwear for British colonialists in tropical climes. During World War I, he came across American soldiers wearing short-sleeved wool underwear. So, he simply combined the idea: a short-sleeved cotton top. It would be decades before underwear turned "outerwear," but a classic was born: today Sunspel still makes its t-shirts, cut for a more tailored fit, and made out of Egyptian cotton to create a long-lasting and super-light garment.

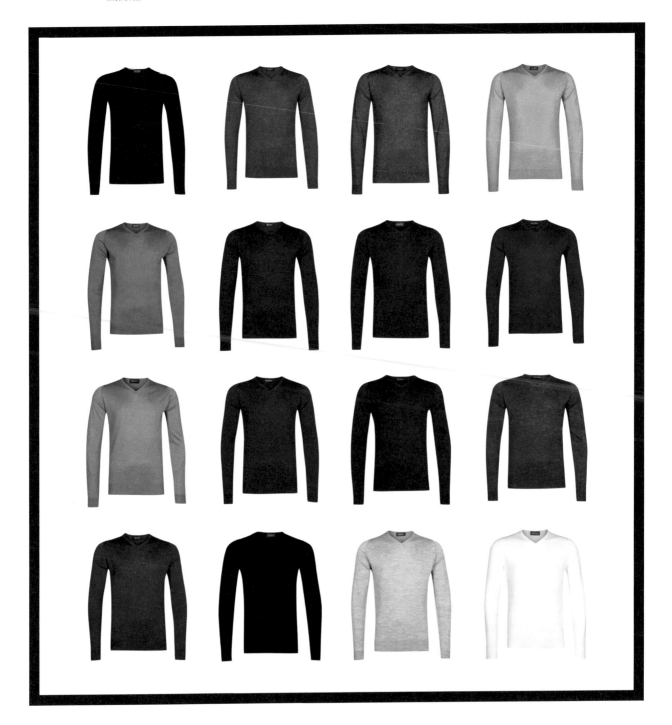

JOHN SMEDLEY

John Smedley, based in Matlock, UK, has some right to claim expertise in fine-gauge knitwear: established in 1784, it is the world's oldest, continually running factory. Its polo shirt, a classic that has been on sale since the 1930s, and its round- and v-neck knits require an intense focus on manufacturing processes and materials: access to spring water, to high-grade wool—the buyer of each Smedley garment can trace the wool used to make it back to the particular sheep farm in New Zealand that supplied it—and to machinery, both high-tech and traditional (some dating to the Victorian period). As such, it has won the Gold Export Award and the British Knitting and Clothing Export Council's Heritage Award (both prestigious within the clothing industry).

KITSUNÉ

The button-down has its origins in 1896 on an English polo field where, in the crowd, one John Brooks, grandson of the founder of Brooks Brothers, noticed that the riders had attached buttons to keep their collar affixed to the main body of the shirt, thus preventing it from flapping into the rider's face. Compared with a business-like, spread shirt collar, the button-down was still smart but relaxed, more bohemian, a preppy icon. But there is always room for improvement: Parisian brand Kitsuné, founded in 2002 by Gildas Loaec and Masaya Kuroki, keeps the classic detailing in place—soft collar, back center box pleat, locker loop and the use of hardwearing Oxford cloth—but to its Italian-made shirts adds contemporary shirt-making touches, like a curved hem and a slimmer fit (since wearers are unlikely to actually want to play polo in theirs).

SANDQVIST

When Anton Sandqvist made his first bag on an old industrial sewing machine, back in 2004, he didn't expect a business to grow out if it. And not a family business either—but Sandqvist was soon joined by his brother Daniel and childhood friend Sebastian Westin, both of whom ran a style magazine at the time. Soon the Stockholm-based company had developed a distinctive, typically Scandinavian style—simple, functional, unfussy—a style in fact very unlike the ugly computer bags that had inspired Anton Sandqvist back when he worked as an engineer. Indeed, the Scandinavian landscape is, inevitably perhaps, inspirational to the brand—the company even has a cabin out in the woods where the trio go to think afresh on new designs. Westin has joked that these designs are inspired by the national "melancholia, so [our designs] become simple or maybe just usable, nothing extravagant or for show—just clean lines and no fun stuff."

FUNCTIONAL

FUNCTIONAL
CLOTHING

TESTED
AND PROVEN

SOLUTION-DRIVEN, PROTECTIVE, AND COMFORTABLE—THAT MAY NOT SOUND VERY ATTRACTIVE. NEVERTHELESS, A HANDFUL OF LABELS ARE CREATING INNOVATIVE SOLUTIONS THAT MASTERFULLY COMBINE FUNCTIONALITY WITH AESTHETICS.

by
JÖRG HAAS

What might first come to mind when thinking of functional clothing are uniforms for the military or police, as well as any kind of workwear. There is also an association with professional sports, especially outdoor activities such as hiking, mountain climbing, snowboarding, or sailing. The common denominator for this type of apparel is a particular design, and respective fabric technologies that meet requirements defined by the field of application and specific climatic conditions. For outdoor use, the sole purpose of a garment is to provide adequate weather protection and comfort, while minimizing constraints such as weight and bulk. The design approach is clearly solution-driven, with a focus on ergonomics and practicality over sheer aesthetics.

In our daily lives, however, it seems as if other standards still apply to the functionality of clothing. Borrowing from "you never get a second chance to make a first impression," the importance seems to lie in the visual signals—the identity/personality conveyed through apparel, whether in a work situation or a private context. Usability and comfort

The majority of us spend a minority of time in challenging situations such as running, climbing, or skiing. Yet we seem more demanding when it comes to the technical capabilities of our athletic gear.

are often neglected for the sake of the aforementioned impression.

Though great technical advancements have been made in the field of textiles and production technologies over the past 20 to 30 years, very few have found their way into our daily lives. The majority of us spend a minority of time in slightly more challenging situations such as running, climbing, or skiing. Yet we seem to demand more when it comes to the technical capabilities of our athletic gear than our regular clothing, which we wear every day and for longer periods. Developing highly functional clothing for the outdoors does seem necessary, as we lack the capability to fully command changing climatic conditions. We need to adapt to nature, rather than adapting the environment to our needs as we do indoors with the use of heating or air conditioning.

Massimo Osti was one of the first to research and produce technically advanced apparel, primarily outerwear. For many designers and enthusiasts, he is the godfather of this category of menswear. His approach, borrowing concepts from

military gear, workwear, and sportswear, has become the common modus operandi for designers following in his footsteps. Osti's legacy continues today in the form of Massimo Osti Studio, which has partnered with outerwear specialist MA.STRUM and the label 12th Man to recreate some of the designer's early graphic works. Ten C, headed by former C.P. Company and Stone Island designers Alessandro Pungetti and Paul Harvey—companies that were both founded by Osti—has been widely recognized for its simplistic style along with the most technically advanced materials. Mostly classic pieces such as the anorak, field jacket, or trench coat have been redesigned with added features to improved versatility or other properties often absent from day-to-day garments.

The design of a technical piece acknowledges ergonomics, climate, and human physiology, but it is the materials—cloth, hardware, insulation—that play a key role in this segment. Technical garments require advanced knowledge during the conceptual process as well as highly specialized fabrication environments, which constitute limiting factors, especially for smaller companies. Thus it is common practice for labels to collaborate with suppliers or large-scale manufacturers; for instance, Japanese brand nanamica works closely with The North Face Japan on all of their technical outerwear. Even among fellow designers, collaborations have become common practice. In recent years, Italian studio Nemen has worked with Scandinavian menswear brand Norse Projects as well as with US/German label Acronym on capsule collections.

The key position regarding materials for use in outerwear is held by W.L. Gore. The Gore-Tex technology, undisputedly the most advanced and well-known technical fabric component, was only just discovered in 1969. Out of frustration, Bob Gore, son of the company's founder William Lee Gore, applied brute force to a heated rod of PTFE (commonly known as Teflon) and happened to expand it to a wafer thin, flexible membrane (expanded PTFE or ePTFE). This material was initially used as insulation for cables; however, its structure proved equally useful for textiles, as water cannot penetrate from the outside, while perspiration can escape through the membrane. The hedge-like structure also shields the wearer from the cooling effects of wind, which is crucial in extreme outdoor activities. The methods of application are as versatile as the membrane's characteristics. It can be integrated into a piece of clothing as a separate liner or directly laminated onto an outer shell. This allows for virtually any kind of fabric to be equipped with weather-protective properties, whether a traditional woolen duffle coat, a corduroy down jacket, or a cotton-faced trench coat.

One of the leading producers of high-end technical apparel is the Austrian company KTC (Knowledge, Technology, and Craft), founded in Hong Kong in 1971. As early as 1981, KTC started producing rainwear for Adidas in its factory in Heshan, located in the southern-Chinese industrial province of Guangdong. Over the years the company has kept pace with technical innovations, becoming one of the most advanced manufacturers of high-end garments in the world. Technological know-how aside, KTC offers complete transparency regarding working conditions, wages, and even economic details, a factor gaining more attention as an indicator for sustainability. In an article for German business magazine Brand Eins, KTC's director, Gerhard Flatz, discusses the production process for just one functional jacket: 65 components (ribbing, buttons, yarns, tape, glues, etc.), together with 216 single fabric parts, are assembled in a process of 520 steps that takes 780 minutes until completion. Adding a $10 profit on top of costs for materials and labor, the production totals $153 for a jacket that retails at $1,000 (including shipping, duties, and the brand's wholesale mark-up). In comparison to a non-technical piece of outerwear consisting of approximately 40–45 components, these numbers are staggering and may explain a reluctance for brands to enter this menswear category.

Since the early 2000s a small group of independent brands has been experimenting with technologies and materials commonly found in the performance sector. At the intersection of personal interest in this field on the part of some designers and a noticeable increase in demand by customers, a new category in menswear has been gradually developing. It can be defined by a design aesthetic that appears to be less fashion-oriented and less seasonal, yet more refined in technical detailing and usability. Therefore, an equally distinct overall style is still present. Two key design currents are predominant: one is heavily influenced by the image of an urban warrior, with references to *Blade Runner* or *Akira;* the other is a more traditional approach whereby classic pieces are updated with modern technology. With their Veilance collection, Canadian outdoor brand Arc'teryx has established a middle ground between these two aesthetics. Notwithstanding the absolute highest level of construction, the design language is neither too overly progressive nor too traditional. With this philosophy, Veilance counterbalances a tendency in functional apparel to aim for the maximum, which is often slightly exaggerated when it comes to daily use. A shirt does not have to look teched-out to provide its wearer with additional features for enhanced comfort.

As much as smaller, progressive brands have been the driving force behind technical/functional innovations in menswear, an equally small circle of knowledgeable retailers has fostered this development and opened the market to a wider audience. One of the earliest supporters of what has recently become the trend is Canadian retailer Haven. Founded by brothers Daniel and Arthur Chmielewski, the first Haven store opened its doors in 2006 in their hometown of Edmonton. Their retail concept was influenced by aesthetic inspiration while traveling through Europe and Japan. From the early streetwear years, Haven's selection has matured with the taste of its owners. A key category for Haven has always been functional apparel, understandably so with the demand for adequate weather protection in Canada's climatic conditions. In addition to its materials, it's in the small details that the overall functionality of an item unfolds over time. Arthur explains: "It's the rear pleats or jersey inserts on your shirt that allow you to be comfortable when reaching for that top bar on a packed metro train. […] It's the extra-large zipper pulls on your bag that allow you to grab your passport from the inner compartment in just a couple seconds. […] These aren't necessarily things you would immediately notice, but things you come to realize later when you're wearing another garment that isn't quite as 'considered.'" The brothers maintain close relationships with the brands and designers they represent. In addition to an in-store service, Haven reaches a global audience through its website and social media channels, offering background information on brands and products through in-depth online features.

Apart from a handful of independents, only a few global corporations have shown heightened interest in functional clothing beyond sportswear. Outerwear remains the predominant category receiving the most attention, even though this type of clothing plays a minor role in our everyday, primarily indoor lives. Developing solutions for other layers such as underwear, shirts, knitwear, or business attire would be a worthy next step.

Slowly but gradually a new category in menswear has been developing. It can be defined by a design aesthetic which appears to be less fashion-orientated, yet more refined in technical detailing.

ACRONYM

Unlike many brands that only recently delved into the world of functional apparel, Acronym has been active in the segment since day one. Michaela Sachenbacher and Errolson Hugh, fellow students at the University of Toronto, founded their design agency in 1994 with a focus on products that unify technology with style. Early clients include Burton Snowboards, who were involved with the main line and sub-labels Analog and iDiom; Arc'teryx Mountain Equipment, the research and development division of W.L. Gore; and the studio of Massimo Osti.

Diverse assignments ranging from sports- and athleticwear to bags and backpacks gave Acronym a chance to gather extensive expertise in various fields such as ergonomics, textile technologies, pattern-making, and production techniques. The concept of enabling enhanced body movement in their designs became a key criterion in the agency's work over the years.

In 1999 Sachenbacher and Hugh launched their own in-house label by the same name as the agency. After three years of research and development, they launched their first product in 2002: the ACRONYM Kit 001. As the name implies, rather than a single piece of outerwear or equipment, a complete package included a jacket, bag, key-ring, belt, CD-ROM, music CD, and comic and instruction manuals.

Kit 001 is a perfect representation of Acronym's design philosophy across all their collections, where items interact with each other in a larger, more complex system. In Kit 001, the shoulder bag was equipped with an external pouch to hold the jacket, and in the event of inclement weather, the jacket could be pulled out with a single hand movement. Without ever taking off the bag, the wearer could slide it under an opening in the jacket for weather protection.

Acronym solves problems with design. Its wearers are equipped with weather protection at the same time that their clothing and bags facilitate the use of modern-day electronics. A collar badge of small magnets, for example, allows earplugs to be stowed when not in use. The Gravity Pocket, integrated into the sleeves of jackets, allows for mobile phones to be stored and accessed easily.

Since its early days of development, Acronym has maintained a close working relationship with W.L. Gore, supplier of the

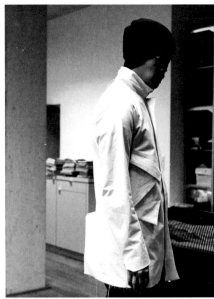

most advanced technical garments. While Gore usually requires that a brand fulfill strict requirements regarding design and fabric use to obtain a license, they were attracted to Acronym's expertise and progressive design approach. And so an almost symbiotic cooperation and the prestigious license for Acronym's own label was attained.

The release of Acronym's Gore-Tex Cashmere GT-J6 jacket in 2004 showcases the advancements of both companies. The standards for the quality of material—a cashmere face equipped with a 3L Gore-Tex membrane—were as high as the design requirements for this innovative textile. Due to its high density, a pattern had to be devised with a maximum of three panels (accounting for six layers of fabric) meeting at any given junction on the jacket. More layering would have caused even the strongest sewing needles to break, as testing had confirmed. This particular piece documents the merits of such a conceptual and collaborative project for the two. While Gore profits from the research and development results that can be passed on to other clients, Acronym as the design partner gains first and exclusive access to newly developed fabrics.

Compared to the size and capabilities of other companies involved in the field of technical/functional menswear, it's an achievement that Acronym has upheld their business model for as long as they have. With a team of less than 10 people in design—and a similar number at their production facility—it is exactly the small-scale of their operation that allows Acronym the flexibility to develop progressive new products expeditiously.

P10-S HD
GABARDINE ARTICULATED
CARGO PANT

Errolson Hugh, cofounder of Acronym, has said that it took him ten years to understand the pant. He goes on to explain the difficulty in finding a design solution that is not restrictive as well as aesthetically pleasing for this foundational garment. Based on the shape of a motocross pant, the P10's cut is narrow. However, its construction—the pattern and seam placement—is laid out to provide maximum movability. Besides a multitude of pockets, the pants' key functionality lies in its material, a high-density cotton gabardine. Developed in England for military use during the Second World War, this natural long-staple cotton fabric is water- and windproof, breathable, and highly durable. After production of this textile ceased during the decline of the British textile industry in the 1990s, Swiss manufacturer Stotz became the official supplier to the British Ministry of Defense. Their EtaProof fabric—as found on the P10—is considered to be the best of its kind.

POLARTECH NTS-NG1 AND CASHMERE KR-SM1 SHEMAG

All of Acronym's products can be seen as tools to successfully deal with varying climatic conditions. By layering garments with different functional characteristics—warming/cooling, insulating, shielding—Acronym produces a small selection of practical accessories to further extend this system. Take a basic product like the tube-like Polartech neck gaiter NTS-NG1. Its highlight comes in the form of the KR-SM1 shemagh, made from 100% pure cashmere wool. Acronym teamed up with a manufacturer in Japan to produce a loose-gauge knit in the desired quality; due to the lightweight construction, it can be stowed in its own small nylon pouch, making it perfect for travel. A cashmere scarf of this quality is most certainly deemed a luxury item. For Acronym, however, this aspect might be considered secondary. The natural fiber's capabilities of both shielding and offering warmth, as well as the material's low volume, were key factors leading to the design and production of this item.

3A-9TS TOTE BAG

Emphasizing the usability aspect of their products, Acronym named its series of bags and backpacks 3rd Arm, or 3A for short. The 3A-9TS is based on the classic canvas tote bag, as made popular by American outdoor retailer L.L. Bean. Acronym offers an enhanced version of this basic style with multiple added features, the most remarkable of which are internal stabilization struts. These keep the bag standing up, even when empty or with a 15-inch laptop stowed in the bag's internal sleeve. For easy use while cycling, a third strap was added to hold it in place, similar to a messenger bag. A fully waterproof zippable top cover keeps contents dry, a feature difficult to find in the average tote bag. Lightweight composite fabric ensures durability and longevity while weight and bulk are kept to a minimum. Though the bag already offers expansive space, its capacity can be extended even further by attaching 3rd Arm accessories: pouches via the outside webbing system.

NANAMICA

the visual signals it conveys. A certain style, a particular accessory, or even a color is a reflection of its wearer's character. The simplest of which could be to look different from everybody else.

When Homma left his outdoor design position to start nanamica, he took the utilitarian design approach and fused it with the requirements of casual fashion aesthetics, developing a brand that, besides being functional, offers a wider range of options and adapts to seasonal changes or trends.

In addition to his technical know-how and a wide-ranging knowledge of sports garments, workwear, and military apparel, Homma has close ties to the textile industry and suppliers of functional fabrics, all of which accounts for nanamica's advantage over competitors. In addition, nanamica works closely with The North Face—the company holds an exclusive license for Japan—and designs its capsule collection "The North Face Purple Label." This relationship not only grants nanamica access to new materials at an early stage, but also guarantees a high level of production quality by sharing The North Face's state-of-the-art manufacturing facilities.

Compared to classic textile manufacturing, requirements for technical

Nanamica's history aligns perfectly with the fluctuation in menswear toward a more sophisticated and grown-up look, a shift that became noticeable in the mid 2000s. Founder Eiichiro Homma had worked in outdoor apparel, specifically marine wear, for 18 years before starting the label in 2003.

Functional apparel is a relatively new category in menswear, roughly two decades old. Many of its designers have a background in outdoor-focused branches of the industry and at one point crossed over into the world of fashion.

It is at this juncture, which Homma has emphasized with his brand, that defining aspects can be carved out. The basic style of a rock-climbing jacket is dictated by purpose-driven requirements that remain unaltered, and thus all brands begin with a shared design similarity. While appearance serves as an identifier for the manufacturer, in fashion, design usually plays the defining role for a piece. Customers demand options according to changing tastes, moods, and trends. So aside from covering basic protective needs, a key functionality of clothing can be seen in

apparel are far more expansive regarding the treatment of fabrics or the ennobling of fibers in a production process. Apart from strict regulations such as W.L. Gore's for the use of its fabrics, a technical apparel brand relies on a manufacturer's capacities and equipment to handle processes such as lamination, seam-taping, or welding.

By cooperating with The North Face, Homma found a strong partner, enabling him to establish nanamica as a niche brand with the technological capabilities of a much larger corporation. In exchange, his design expertise provides The North Face's main activewear line with an infusion of design concepts aimed at a more fashion-focused consumer.

Looking at both projects, it is hard to draw a clear line distinguishing the two when it comes to the outdoor and casual-/dailywear categories. A nanamica jacket might take the shape of a classic mountain parka, fully equipped with the latest Gore-Tex fabric technology, but with colors apt for the urban landscape. The North Face Purple Label Snow-Anorak, a classic outdoor piece, might feature a vintage chambray paisley-pattern fabric commonly used for shirting.

Nanamica and The North Face Purple Label both offer functional menswear collections, namely outerwear, complemented by cut and sew items, accessories, and bags. While the approach toward design and production may seem strict, the varying themes in seasonal releases showcase a flexibility that the consumer of casual menswear/fashion demands. These brands embody an innovative spirit that lies in their willingness to apply design principles as well as relatively new technologies to an otherwise traditional segment.

NANAMICA/
THE NORTH FACE
PURPLE LABEL

While The North Face offers their main collection globally, the company also operates under license in Japan, producing additional goods exclusively for the regional market. The North Face Purple Label, exclusive to Japan, is a seasonal capsule collection. With a design aesthetic that borrows from outdoor apparel, the collection is meant for use in a non-performance, more urban casual context. The featured crew neck sweater is knit in a pattern reminiscent of traditional, often colorful Scandinavian designs, but is executed in plain blue or white. On the chest, a buttoned flap pocket is attached, a detail common to military issue sweaters. The use of Coolmax yarn, a mix of natural and synthetic fibers, provides increased comfort. When worn next-to-skin, this fabric is highly breathable and quick-drying due to its moisture-wicking capability. As with many items from The North Face Purple Label, this crew neck sweater epitomizes their philosophy of updating a classic style with modern elements and fabric technologies.

WHITE MOUNTAINEERING

Yosuke Aizawa traces the inspiration to start his White Mountaineering label back to childhood camping trips with his dad. He remembers a fascination with the outdoor apparel his dad ordered for both of them from the U.S. After working for Junya Watanabe in the more artistic context of apparel design, Aizawa decided to launch his own project with a more pragmatic direction in 2006. The French Linen Trench perfectly showcases his approach to menswear; materials are not just chosen for their aesthetic appeal but also for their functionality. While the natural fabric on the face of this coat has no technical capabilities, the inside, a Gore-Tex Paclite membrane, provides full weather protection without adding extra bulk to the garment. The stark contrast between the blue dye of the natural linen exterior and the neutral gray color of the synthetic, highly technical interior accounts for the peculiar aesthetic of this hybrid between traditional coat and high-performance shell.

STONE ISLAND

As much a designer as a researcher, Massimo Osti, founder of Stone Island, was central to the evolution of functional modern menswear. From the beginning of his career, Osti was amassing a huge archive of apparel, jackets, workwear, protective, and military clothing. He was also collecting fabrics and material samples that gave him detail and design inspiration for his own work. This constant study and his progressive approach toward material innovation led to the launch of Stone Island in 1982, when Osti experimented with a waterproof fabric commonly used for military trucks. Fascinated by its characteristics, Osti devised a multi-cycle treatment to break down the fabric's structure, making it suitable for outerwear production while retaining its water-resistance. Too progressive an execution for his existing label, C.P. Company, Osti launched the collection—seven jackets produced entirely in the new fabric, Tela Stella—as Stone Island. The name pays tribute to the nautical-themed novels of Joseph Conrad and is a reference to the stonewash treatment of the first fabric. A badge featuring a compass, similar to military insignia, was placed on the exterior of the garments and has remained unchanged since the brand's inception.

After Massimo Osti's departure from Stone Island in 1993 (he died in 2005 from severe illness), Carlo Rivetti, a shareholder from the company's early

days, together with his sister, bought out the firm. Renaming it Sportswear Company, Rivetti has served as Stone Island's creative director since. Paul Harvey, who worked for legendary German tech-apparel label Sabotage in the mid 1990s, became head designer in 1996 and went on to design 24 collections during his 12-year stay at the label. Rivetti's creative direction, Harvey's design language, and the company's unconventional research and development processes have resulted in some truly iconic pieces of apparel that, apart from outerwear, include knitwear, pants, shirts, bags, footwear, and accessories.

What sets Stone Island apart from other clothing companies as a leader in the industry is a limitless motivation for innovation. Aside from sourcing

materials outside the realm of conventional textile manufacturing, the company operates its own research facility to conceive new fabrics, dyes, and treatment processes. They also have a laboratory where formulas and treatments are tested and applied during the finishing stages of production. Functionality is interpreted as how a specific characteristic of a dye or coating—a treatment in general—functions with a fabric, but also what functionalities the finished piece offers its wearer.

In 2008 Stone Island started an ongoing collaboration with design studio Acronym to create the sub-label Shadow Project. With a focus on functionality, Stone Island ventured even further into the field of technical apparel. Categorized within a system of interacting pieces of clothing called PARSEQ (Proof, Augment, Resist, Skin, and Equip), each item in a collection, be it jackets, insulation, knitwear, or bags, is designed to interact with one another, even across different seasons. In addition to this functionality across categories, Shadow Project's pieces offer additional functionalities on their own. Pants or shorts are equipped with hidden cargo pockets, scarves feature snap buttons to work as collar extensions on jackets, and coats are constructed with detachable layers to adapt to changing climates.

While Stone Island's main line is characterized by its bright color palette and bold effects, the Shadow Project offers a subtler take on modern menswear. Together, they offer a progressive attitude towards functionality, fabric technologies, and overall design aesthetics.

STONE ISLAND
MARINA

As the name suggests, Stone Island Marina is a maritime-themed capsule collection within the label's main line. Generally, the color palette is limited to black, navy, or white, and the garments feature only subtle branding in the form of glow-in-the-dark prints or labeling. Apart from apparel that includes jackets, knitwear, and trousers, Marina also encompasses a series of functional bags. Their Dry Bag is produced by Ortlieb, a German manufacturer well-known for highly functional bicycle and travel equipment bags. The ultra-resistant PVC fabric on the sides and the nylon canvas on the top are both 100 percent waterproof. In combination with the water- and air-tight zip fastening, contents will stay dry—empty and inflated, the bag could even serve as an emergency flotation device. In addition to the diagonal shoulder strap, the two carry handles allow the bag to be worn as a backpack for better weight distribution.

WTAPS

The brand WTAPS was founded in 1996 by Tetsu Nishiyama. He belongs to a small group of independent Tokyo-based designers, among them Hiroshi Fujiwara, Jun Takahashi, and Nigo (founder of A Bathing Ape). In the mid-1990s they laid the foundation for a young and progressive fashion-design movement, which over the past two decades has been enjoying growing global recognition. Nishiyama draws inspiration from vintage military apparel, mainly 1960s Vietnam-era pieces, sometimes reproducing a style almost identically to its original. Similar to a watch cap used by the U.S. Navy, the Coolmax Beanie is a modern update, knit with a yarn of cotton and Coolmax fiber. Lightweight and with additional moisture-management capabilities, the beanie is a versatile accessory for the spring or cooler summer days; a heavier construction is available for the fall.

ARC'TERYX

Arc'teryx's history began in a garage in Vancouver, Canada, where in 1989 climber Dave Lane, unhappy with what was available on the market, started developing his own mountain gear. Lane, together with his business partner Jeremy Guard, introduced a series of improved products under the brand name Rock Solid. The first series included the 3D-sculpted climbing harness Vapor. This piece of equipment encompasses the company's unorthodox design approach to delivering innovative products based on extensive research. Their work has resulted in numerous advancements in the field of outdoor equipment and functional apparel, many of which have become industry standards. In 1991 the company was renamed Arc'teryx, short for archaeopteryx, symbolizing the evolutionary struggle for improvement.

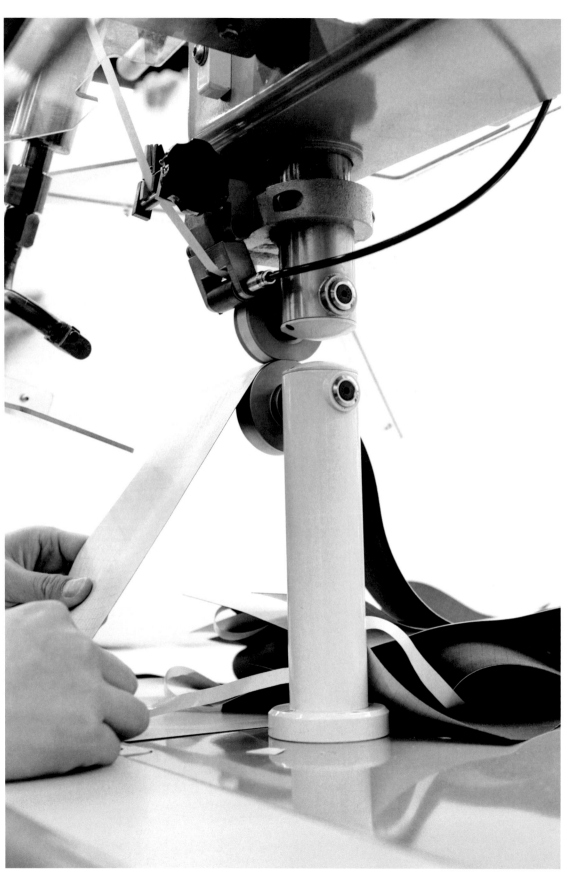

The Vapor harness—still in production today—led the way for design details that are still found on a multitude of products. Its 3D-design, for example, was achieved by experimenting with industrial foams and the process of thermoforming. In order to reduce bulk while still improving strength and stability, layers of fabric were laminated instead of being sewn together. Not only did the Vapor introduce a much lighter harness than any available on the market at the time, but it was also more ergonomic, more durable, and longer lasting.

A new chapter in innovation began in 1996 when Arc'teryx acquired a license from W.L. Gore for the use of Gore-Tex fabrics for outerwear. Technologies that

had previously been applied to hard goods were now transferred onto apparel. Jackets and trousers feature articulated sleeve- and leg-designs for improved mobility, and pockets or collars were attached using lamination and welding processes to reduce weight and bulk. Certainly, one of Arc'teryx most outstanding technical novelties is the watertight zipper. Rarely is a piece of outerwear or equipment seen without it today.

Arc'teryx's design innovations are triggered by a motivation to conceive better products for specific uses. In the early 2000s Arc'teryx observed an appropriation of its outdoor apparel in urban environments, thus identifying a consumer demand for the daily use of

functional outerwear. The initial concept for an urban line of apparel was conceived in 2003, but it was not until 2010 that this project was realized as Arc'teryx Veilance.

While outdoor garments are designed for one specific activity in a defined climate—think climbing, skiing, or snowboarding—the urban landscape confronts a wearer with constantly changing settings: indoor vs. outdoor, car vs. public transportation, formal vs. informal, office vs. private space. Veilance's aim is to offer designs, as well as technical solutions, to cope with these multifaceted requirements. In addition, a new challenge has been presented for Arc'teryx as aesthetics play a more prominent and defining role in this apparel category.

Even though Veilance releases two collections per year, the brand does not necessarily offer new styles. In most cases, the extended research and development phases do not allow for a quick turnover, as designing a multifunctional piece can take several months. Thus, a successful new style is carried over several seasons, with a focus on continued improvement. Unlike conventional menswear brands, Veilance's designs are dictated by requirements and problem-solving rather than seasonal changes and the newest themes and concepts.

Similar to Arc'teryx's outerwear, which redefined the aesthetics of mountainwear through its subtle, low-key appearance, the Veilance line established a new category of functional menswear with its muted colors, neutral silhouettes, and non-existent branding. Traditional pieces such as blazers or coats are reengineered from the bottom up rather than reproduced in modern fabrics. Built from Arc'teryx's technical expertise, these pieces carry the same spirit as the classic styles they are based on, but constitute a new form of clothing altogether.

ARC'TERYX VEILLANCE

VORONOI PANT

The Voronoi Pant by Arc'teryx Veilance is an exemplary piece to demonstrate the brand's practice of reengineering staple apparel pieces to enhance wear comfort. The key feature on these pants is the articulated design of the legs, which becomes visible when laid flat on the side. Following the anatomy of the leg, the cut of the Voronoi is slightly bent. Seams are strategically placed to support the flowing effect of the garment when worn. In combination with the stretchable nylon fabric, this construction—loosely based on the mathematical Voronoi diagrams—ensures ease of wear and unrestricted movement. These versatile pants are ideal when traveling, not only due to water- and wind-resistance and low volume, but also reduced weight and bulk. The Voronoi Pant is a hybrid: wear as a formal pant for business meetings with a dress shirt and the matching Blazer; or, head outdoors on a hike and the pant becomes perfectly casual.

BLAZER LT

Figuratively speaking, the Arc'teryx Veilance Blazer LT is a piece of performance outerwear disguised as a semiformal sports coat. As is often the case in the functional apparel category, the absence of details more than the abundance thereof accounts for the quality of a garment. Devoid of otherwise key elements such as hood, exterior pockets, storm front, and zip, the focus lies on the material choice—in this case a performance stretch fabric that offers basic weather resistance. To further improve the jacket's protective capabilities the seams are taped, and with the laminated lapel forward and collar folded up, even slightly harsher conditions can be mastered. This piece is especially handy for travel, as it is packable, crease-resistant, low-maintenance, and offers zippered pockets to stow documents, phone, and other essentials. Pairing the Blazer LT with the Voronoi Pant makes for an interesting, advanced, and highly functional business suit.

COMPONENT SHIRT

The design of the Arc'teryx Veilance Component Shirt follows the concept of body mapping. Various fabrics are combined on one garment so that their particular functionalities correspond with the different climatic zones of the human body. Made from a fully breathable nylon/cotton poplin fabric, the front panel of this shirt is refined with a water repellant and is stretchable for enhanced comfort. The back of the shirt features a merino wool knit panel. The natural fiber's characteristics—it is highly moisture-wicking, antibacterial, fully breathable, and adaptive to varying temperatures (either cooling or warming)—are perfectly utilized for the high overall thermal output of this body region. Gusseted underarms offer additional ventilation. On par with the Veilance aesthetic, the Component Shirt appears as a hybrid suitable for more formal contexts when paired with matching Veilance Trousers and Blazer. But it can certainly be worn casually too.

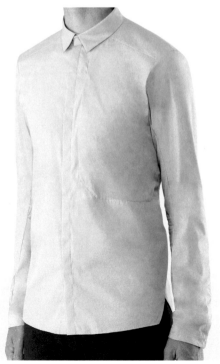

MISSION WORKSHOP

THE DIVISION CHINO

While known for their line of functional bags, backpacks, and accessories targeting the active consumer, Mission Workshop also offers a capsule apparel collection consisting of merino wool knitwear, outerwear, and pants. With their clean silhouettes and subtle color palette of grays and blacks, all garments are suitable for various occasions whether formal or casual. The Division Chino is produced in Dryskin, a technical fabric by Swiss manufacturer Schoeller. As the name suggests, this material's key characteristic is its moisture management capability. Additionally, Dryskin is treated with Nanosphere, Schoeller's patented water repellant, and offers enhanced movability due to its four-way stretch capacity. Equally important is the durability of this particular fabric, when considering the increased wear-and-tear effects of cycling. With this material choice, Mission Workshop acknowledges that other than a jacket, pants must stand up to all-day wear in varying conditions.

VX / R8 MODULAR
ARKIV FIELD BACKPACK

The founders of San Francisco–based Mission Workshop all have a cycling background. Their extensive experiences on two wheels lie at the core of the company's product development. Take the R8 Field pack, the most versatile of their backpacks. An external rail system—patented under the name Arkiv— allows for the attachment of various accessories depending on use. There are a number of pouches in different sizes and formats as well as specific options such as a notebook sleeve, tool pouch, or document organizer. Some smaller bags are also equipped with rails to extended their capacity even further. To keep contents dry, the Cordura nylon ripstop shell is backed with a waterproof Teflon membrane in addition to its nylon lining. All components, particularly in combination, make for a highly durable overall construction that withstand demanding conditions. Even in its basic form, this backpack offers numerous compartments and functional details to facilitate usage.

VISVIM

One season it might be a full-size Teepee, the next an original U.S. 1960s camping trailer. Then, the Buckminster Fuller geodesic dome or a four-meter-high road sign of young Ronald Reagan as a cowboy. Centerpieces such as these were sourced and shipped to Paris from all corners of the world for Visvim's seasonal presentations. While these artifacts are representations of the collections' themes, they also serve as an introduction to the label's design philosophy and modus operandi of its creative director Hiroki Nakamura. If Nakamura readily has several hundred kilos of raw buffalo hide as well as corresponding poles hauled across continents simply for decorative purposes, it is easy to imagine the challenges he is willing to take on as a designer and manufacturer of artisanal collections. There are no limitations or compromises in sight.

What started as a footwear brand in Japan in 2001 has evolved over the years into a global luxury lifestyle brand. Covering various footwear categories and offering men's and women's apparel, it also features bags, accessories, jewelry, cosmetics, homeware, and even coffee. Visvim keeps expanding its portfolio while constantly pushing the boundaries of today's manufacturing processes. Based on the principles of a research and development laboratory, the brand strives to deliver the best possible products and services to its costumers. Visvim's flagship stores are aptly named F.I.L. (Free International Laboratory).

Nakamura is an avid collector of vintage clothing. He takes inspiration from century-old fabrics, patterns, and cuts, but also examines functional characteristics of traditional, sometimes archaic, garments and footwear. The findings of his research are often documented in the brand's elaborate collection catalogs. In Dissertations on the Future Relationship Between Materials and Technologies in Product Fundamentalism Vol. 2 (Fall/Winter 2008/2009), Nakamura describes his encounter with a Sami tribes woman introducing him to the ancient craft of shoemaking. Combining the natural properties of reindeer leather (breathable, moisture-absorbing) with untreated hay as insulation (air pockets in between strands retain heat), their style of boot—unchanged for centuries—offers unparalleled protection in the harsh conditions of Lapland. Discoveries such as this led Nakamura to develop a line of footwear labeled Folk, which features untreated leather uppers, cork footbeds, and bamboo inserts for cushioning.

At first sight, the style of Nakamura's designs, the objects he displays in his shops, or the accessories complementing his collections can be misconstrued. Vintage is the obvious theme: vintage cars, vintage furniture, vintage kimonos, vintage folk art. However, unlike many Japanese brands that take pride in reproducing vintage clothing down to the last detail, Nakamura's aim is to learn from such archival pieces to then update them. Applying state-of-the-art technology, fabric properties are enhanced for modern-day use. The cut of Visvim's Commodore coat, for example, is based on the classic British dufflecoat. It is offered in Harris Tweed, though the traditional woolen fabric is enhanced by a 3L Gore-Tex membrane, offering even further weather protection.

Fusing the traditional with the modern has also led Nakamura in the opposite direction. Having discovered the ancient craft of natural dyeing—indigo, mud, cochineal—he applied such techniques to modern fabrics, as found on a 3L Gore-Tex jacket from Visvim's 2013 Fall/Winter collection. After a lengthy manual dyeing process in either natural indigo or mud, each piece displays individual characteristics, creating a handcrafted effect on this otherwise highly technical, functional garment. Due to the limitations in fabrics, for example vintage indigo-dyed Kimono fabrics or U.S.-sourced patchwork blankets, production runs are often minuscule and prices astronomical.

ACHILLES SOCKS

For many of its footwear styles, Visvim uses vegetable-tanned leathers without additional finishes to keep the breathability of the material intact. For its Folk line in particular, Visvim even encourages wearers not to put on socks to make full use of the leathers' natural moisture-management capabilities. If they must, however, the brand also offers socks in various lengths and color combinations. The common denominator of all Achilles Socks is the use of Dralon yarn, produced by the German manufacturer of the same name, in combination with cotton. By balancing out both fibers' inherent range of functionalities, these socks offer a level of comfort usually only found in high-performance sports products. They are antibacterial and extremely moisture-wicking, durable and also easily washed at low temperatures. The yarn is colorfast and will retain its brightness. The latter is especially important for Visvim, a highly design-driven company that takes pride in offering long-lasting products.

FBT AND PATRICIAN WT FOLK

The sneaker-moccasin hybrid FBT, named after British band Fun Boy Three, whose lead singer Terry Hall favored this footwear style, put Visvim on the map with its 2001 launch. A popular style ever since, Hiroki Nakamura has reengineered the midsole with an ultra-light EVA Phylon construction commonly found in performance shoes, while keeping the shoes' upper design almost identical to its Native-American counterpart. Over the years, updating classic silhouettes with technologically advanced materials has been a recurring theme in Visvim's collections, seen in their hiking boots, penny loafers, and this alteration of the classic Brogue. On the Patrician WT Folk, the characteristic perforated leather panels are kept in their original format. Instead of a leather sole, however, an abrasion-resistant, ultra-lightweight Vibram sole is used to reduce the shoe's weight and offer increased cushioning. Further improvements include a natural cork footbed and bamboo shank for added comfort.

FUNCTIONAL
JACKETS

Functionality in apparel has many different facets. There are functional fabrics that offer enhanced comfort, are versatile in use, and require little maintenance. The cut of a garment is functional when it provides greater movability and adaptability in different contexts. Colors, materials, and the appearance of a piece of clothing convey visual signals—a key sociological functionality. Furthermore, sustainability and recyclability are functional aspects that have gained more recognition in recent years.

One category in menswear that has seen notable advancements regarding modern technology is outerwear, jackets in particular. A jacket is the first, thus most important barrier to shield its wearer from unfavorable weather conditions.

Over the past 20 to 30 years, more and more aspects of performance wear have found their way into garments designed for daily use. In addition to new materials with added capabilities, modern production technologies such as laser cutting, seam welding, or ultra sonic bonding have created new opportunities for more functional garments. Digital printing as well as new dyes and coatings add a wide range of novel possibilities for progressive apparel design.

In general, jackets can be subdivided into various categories based on their intended use within various climates and seasons. A direct reference to outdoor apparel is the idea of layering. The combination of an insulator and a shell offers a spectrum of uses for changing

weather conditions. While a thinner outer jacket—a bonded fabric featuring a protective membrane (Gore-Tex, Pertex, Toray)—solely shields against wind and water, the insulator—down or synthetic padding such as Coreloft or Primaloft—provides warmth. Ideally, the various layers complement each other, allowing for a balanced system of ventilation, moisture management, warming, or cooling.

The light shell is a relatively new subcategory in outerwear. This packable, ultra-lightweight garment offers basic weather protection for shorter periods of time. The shell is perfect when commuting, passing through different microclimates within an urban environment, or while weathering unstable climatic conditions.

STONE ISLAND

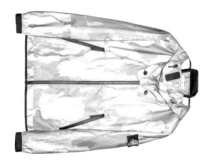

NORSE PROJECTS

WTAPS

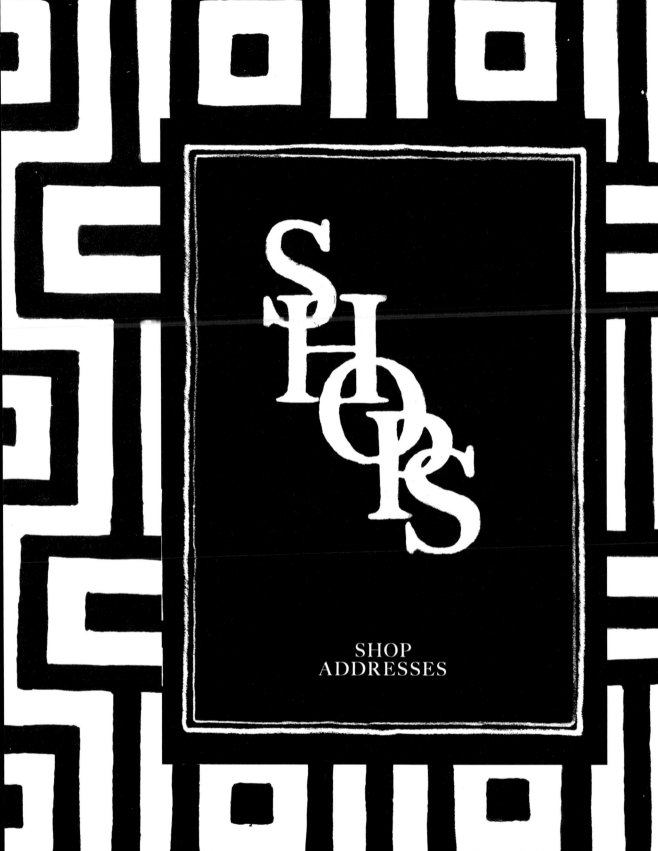

SHOPS

SHOP
ADDRESSES

THE ARMOURY
307 Pedder Building,
12 Pedder Street Central,
Hong Kong

RIVET & HIDE
5 Windmill Street,
London W1T 2JA, UK

LE RAYON FRAIS
11/13/15 Rue St James,
33000 Bordeaux, France

BURG & SCHILD
Rosa-Luxemburg-Strasse 3,
10178 Berlin, Germany

BURG & SCHILD (BERLIN)

LEFFOT
10 Christopher St.,
NYC 10014, New York, USA

THE FINE DANDY SHOP
445 West 49th Street, Hell's Kitchen,
NYC 10019, New York, USA

VMC ORIGINAL
Rindermarkt 8,
8001 Zürich, Switzerland

CHELSEA FARMERS CLUB
Schlüterstrasse 50,
10629 Berlin, Germany

HAVEN
52 East Cordova Street,
Vancouver, BC V6A 1K2, Canada

MAKING THINGS
Geroldstrasse 23,
8005 Zurich, Switzerland

FIRMAMENT
Linienstrasse 40,
10119 Berlin, Germany

THE STANDARD STORE
503 Crown Street, Surry Hills,
NSW 2010, Sidney, Australia

HAVEN (TORONTO)

333
Borgo Giacomo Tommasini 12,
43121 Parma, Italy

ODIN
199 Lafayette Street,
New York, USA

VOO STORE
Oranienstrasse 24,
10999 Berlin, Germany

MATCHES
13 Hill Street, Richmond,
London TW9 1SX, UK

BEYMEN
Abdi İpekçi Caddesi No:23/1,
İstanbul, Turkey

PRESENT
140 Shoreditch High Street,
London E1 6JE, UK

BIOTOP
4-6-44 Shirokanedai, Minato-ku,
Tokyo, Japan

ONLINE
www.mrporter.com
www.gilt.com
www.cultizm.com
www.coggles.com

VOO STORE (BERLIN)

MERCI
111 Boulevard Beaumarchais,
75003 Paris, France

THESE
SHOP ADDRESSES
ARE RECOMMENDED BY
THE EDITORS.

AP & CO
Talstrasse 58,
8001 Zürich, Switzerland

INDEX

COUNTRYSIDE

FRANK LEDER
Photo Credit: Gregor Hohenberg
Pages 18–21

INIS MEÁIN
Photo Credit: Matthew Thompson
Pages 22–25

AIGLE
Von Schöning PR
Pages 26–29

GRENSON
Page 30

GUDRUN & GUDRUN
Sane Communications London
Page 31

HOLLAND & HOLLAND
Page 32

HUNTER
Page 33

BARBOUR
Pages 34–37

SCOTT-NICHOL
Photo Credit: www.adtrak.co.uk
Pantherella
Page 38

STUTTERHEIM
Photo Credit: Mikael Olsson (top),
Erik Lefvander (middle),
Ambrose Leung (bottom)
Agency V
Page 39

LOCK & CO. HATTERS
Page 40

ROECKL
Page 41

WOLFEN
Photo Credit: Zoé Beausire
Page 42

YUKETEN
Photo Credit: Saki Sato
Meg Company
Page 43

FORMAL

RICHARD JAMES
Pages 48–49

TURNBULL & ASSER
Photo Credits: Origin Films (p. 50),
Andy Barnham (pp. 51–52),
David Calderley (p. 53)
Pages 50–53

ISAAC REINA
Photo Credit: Carles Roig
Pages 54–55

BARENA
Stylist: Massimo Pigozzo
Photo Credit: Antonio Piarotto
Page 56

DUCHAMP
Stylist: Simon Foxton
Photo Credit: Nick Griffiths
Page 57

CROMBIE
Page 58

CHRISTY'S HATS
Page 59

E.TAUTZ
Photo Credit: Nick Andrews
Page 60

E. MARINELLA
Photo Credit: Roberto Sorrentino
Page 61

STEPHAN SCHNEIDER
Photo Credit: Kira Bunse (p. 62),
Joachim Müller Ruchholtz (p. 63)
Pages 62–63

ANDERSON'S
Page 64

HACKETT
Page 65

LUDWIG REITER
Photo Credit: Gerd Kressl
Pages 66–67

PANTHERELLA
Photo Credit: Linda Blann
Page 68

CHEANEY
Joseph Cheaney & Son
Page 69

FESTIVE

PAUL STUART
Courtesy of Paul Stuart
Pages 74–77

GIEVES & HAWKES
Pages 78–81

GAZIANO & GIRLING
Photo Credits: Peter Haynes (pp. 83, 84–85),
Luke Carby (82, 83)
Pages 82–85

CHARVET
Pages 86–89

DOYLE MUESER
Photo Credits: Rose Callahan (left),
Zhi Wie (right)
Page 90

JEFFREY-WEST
Page 91

DENTS
Photo Credit: Gemma Willmore
Pages 92–93

D.S. & DURGA
Pages 94–95

BY ELIAS
Photo Credit: Bevin Elias
Page 96

FOX UMBRELLAS
Page 97

SECRET EMPIRE
Photo Credit: Jen McBride
Page 98

POST IMPERIAL
Photo Credit: Lakin Ogunbawo
Page 99

CARUSO
Page 100

DRAKE'S
Photo Credit: Jamie Ferguson
Page 101

CORGI
Page 102

NACKYMADE
Photo Credit: Norikazu Sakamoto
Page 103

HVRMINN & CO.
Photo Credit: Bon Duke
Page 104

LAIRD HATTERS
Page 105

LE LOIR EN PAPILLON
Photo Credits: Massimiliano Mocchia di Coggiola
(p. 106 top), Virginie Le Gall (p. 106 top middle, 108 top,
109), Le Loir en Papillon (p. 106 middle bottom),
Marie-Camille Raynaud (p. 106 bottom), Marie-Paola
Bertrand-Hillion (p. 107), Mickael Cornelus (p. 108 bottom)
Pages 106–109

ACTIVE

OUTLIER
Photo Credits: Liam Quigley (pp. 114–115, 119),
Emiliano Granado (pp. 116–117, 119),
Joshua Pestka (p. 118)
Pages 114–119

SEIL MARSCHALL
Pages 120–121

ORLEBAR BROWN
LOEWS GmbH
Pages 122–125

JOHN ELLIOTT + CO
Photo Credit: Patrick Maus
Page 126

LYLE & SCOTT
Page 127

PENFIELD
Sane Communications London
Page 128

RAF SIMONS X ADIDAS
häberlein & mauerer
Page 129

RAPHA
Pages 130–131

DAN WARD
Photo Credit: Mattia Tacconi
Page 132

CHAMPION X NANAMICA
nanamica inc.
Page 133

FROM TIP TO TOE
The Essential Men's Wardrobe

IMPRINT

This book was conceived, edited and designed by Gestalten.

Edited by Robert Klanten and Sven Ehmann
Preface by Duncan Campbell

Chapter introductions and portraits written by:
Nathaniel Adams (pp. 70–109),
Josh Sims (pp. 44–69, 152–161, 164–165, 171–213),
Omar Muñoz Cremers (pp. 14–43, 111–143, 170),
Jörg Haas (pp. 214–245),
Robin van der Kaa (pp. 148–151, 162–163, 166–169)

Design and typography by BUREAU Mario Lombardo
Editorial management by Vanessa Obrecht
Illustrations by Daavid Mörtl
Cover photography by Bruno Ehrs for Gieves & Hawkes
Proofreading by Transparent Language Solutions

Typefaces: Arrow, Brown, BUREAU Caslon,
BUREAU Grid, BUREAU Plakat,
Didot, Florentine, Futura,
Times New Roman, Trade Gothic

Printed by Nino Druck GmbH, Neustadt/Weinstr.
Made in Germany

Published by Gestalten, Berlin 2015
ISBN: 978-3-89955-568-4

Bibliographic information published
by the Deutsche Nationalbibliothek.
The Deutsche Nationalbibliothek lists this
publication in the Deutsche Nationalbibliografie;
detailed bibliographic data are
available online at http://dnb.d-nb.de.

None of the content in this book was
published in exchange for payment by
commercial parties or designers;
Gestalten selected all included work
based solely on its artistic merit.

This book was printed on paper certified to the standard of FSC®.

MIX
Paper from
responsible sources
FSC® C006655